God's Wisdom for Young People Today

The advice given in the book of Proverbs is as applicable today as it was in the days of Solomon.

Think of these daily devotions from Proverbs and other parts of the Bible as **spiritual vitamins**—God's thoughts in bite-sized pieces. One a day will help you steadily build your endurance and your understanding.

Subjects include: God's wisdom versus the wisdom of the world; use of time and other resources; wisdom at home and with friends; wisdom of learning, self-discipline, instruction and much more.

Six daily readings each week for twelve weeks.

MILES AHEAD

DAILY DEVOTIONS BASED ON GOD'S WISDOM

MILES AHEAD

DAILY DEVOTIONS BASED ON GOD'S WISDOM

COMPILED BY **RICK BUNDSCHUH**

EDITED BY **CAROL BOSTROM**

Regal Books

A Division of GL Publications
Ventura, CA U.S.A.

Miles Ahead
A Devotional Guide to God's Wisdom
Compiled by Rick Bundschuh
Edited by Carol Bostrom
Illustrated by Tom Finley

The translation of all Regal books is under the direction of GLINT. GLINT provides technical help for the adaptation, translation and publishing of books for millions of people worldwide. For information regarding translation contact: GLINT, P.O. Box 6688, Ventura, California 93006.

Published by Regal Books
A Division of GL Publications
Ventura, California 93006
Printed in U.S.A.

Library of Congress Cataloging in Publication Data

Main entry under title:

Miles ahead.
1. Bible. O.T. Proverbs—Meditations. I. Bundschuh, Rick, 1951- . II. Bostrom, Carol.
BS1465.4.M55   1984   223'.706   84-4784
ISBN 0-8307-0950-9 (pbk.)

Contents

Author
Information

The following people contributed to this collection of devotions:

Todd Alexander is high school coordinator for Forest Home Christian Conference Center, Forest Falls, California. He is responsible for planning, organizing and supervising all programming for high school conferences, as well as assisting in other program areas such as family camp.

Carol Bostrom is editor of youth curriculum at Gospel Light Publications, Ventura, California, writer of a number of study guides and other educational materials, and well-known for her ability to laugh at other people's jokes.

Brent Bromstrup is associate pastor of youth and missions at Barrington Baptist Church, Barrington, Rhode Island. He describes himself as a professional bald person.

Rick Bundschuh is youth editor (sometimes known as youth czar) at Gospel Light Publications, a heavy surfer, a much-published cartoonist and writer ("Maynard and the Rat" in *Surfer* magazine), and co-producer of the film *Good Clean Fun!*

David Edwards, a free-lance writer who lives in a converted barn in Ojai, California, is best known for his two LPs on the Myrrh Records label *(David Edwards, Get the Picture)*. David's articles have appeared in magazines such as *Windstorm* and *Contemporary Christian Music Magazine*. He is the author of an essay on religious music and poetry called "The Devout Masque," a gourmet cook, and an avid collector of books.

Tom Finley is senior designer for high school curriculum at Gospel Light, Ventura, California, and author of *Diabolus Seeks Revenge* and *Wilbur, Master of the Rats*. He does the drawing for the cartoon "Maynard and the Rat" in *Surfer* magazine, and is often seen checking out the waves.

Susan Hansen is a wife and homemaker. She spends her time chasing her two toddlers and working with the junior high leadership team and women's ministries in her church in Kent, Washington. When people ask her when she finds time to do her free-lance writing, she laughingly says, "In my free time."

Jan Johnson is a free-lance curriculum writer. She is a partner to her husband as he ministers in urban and cross-cultural settings. They presently live in Inglewood, California. With two preschool children at home, Jan divides her time between typing and washing crayon off the walls.

Ed Stewart is associate pastor at Evergreen Christian Center in Hillsboro, Oregon. He and his wife are perpetually surrounded by teenagers. Recently over a two-year period they served as foster parents to about 40 Vietnamese teenagers. Presently they live with a Brazilian foreign exchange student and their own 16-year-old daughter and 18-year-old son. In addition, Ed has a number of involvements with the young people at his church.

Two Kinds of Wisdom

Day 1 Wisdom from God's Perspective

Shelly races down the hall to her algebra class. Oops! There goes the bell. Late again! Puffing hard, she tries to slip unobtrusively into her seat, but Mr. Suarez notices and sends a frown in her direction as he marks her tardy.

Bells. Schedules. Clocks. Calendars. Who needs them? Just about all of us. Teachers need to know how much time they have to teach a lesson. Airline passengers need some assurance that they will reach their destination at the planned time. Customers want to know what time a store will be open.

But there are people who don't appreciate schedules or rules of any sort. These people feel that their freedom is inhibited by guidelines. So it's a matter of perspective whether you appreciate a rule because it helps you, or resent it because it hampers your life-style.

Perspective is an important concept in many areas. For an artist, a grasp of perspective is necessary in order to make a landscape appear realistic. For a person seeking to live a fulfilled and productive life, it is important to look at things from God's perspective. For God has the wisdom needed to produce such a life.

But there are counterfeits that can confuse us. The world system around us offers us its own so-called wisdom—but "the wisdom of this world is foolishness in God's sight" (1 Cor. 3:19). People assume that they have the wisdom to make their own decisions, but Proverbs 14:12 tells us that "there is a way that seems right to a man, but in the end it leads to death." We do not have God's perspective of wisdom and we cannot understand things as He does. Actions that seem wise to people are foolish to God: they don't make any sense. Since God's perspective is perfect, it is we who have to revise our thinking about wisdom.

When we realize that human wisdom is foolishness to God, we are more willing to accept the advice of the apostle Paul. He warns us not to be deceived; if anyone thinks himself wise "*by the standards of this age,* he should become a 'fool' so that he may become wise" (1 Cor. 3:18, emphasis added). We need to look for God's perspective in our pursuit of wisdom.

Does your perspective on wisdom matter to you? How can considering wisdom from God's point of view affect your life today and in the future?

In Proverbs 24:1-4 two perspectives are described. Read these verses and compare the results of pursuing wisdom versus pursuing wickedness.

Day 2 Spiritual Wisdom

A ballad called "Scarlet Ribbons" tells the story of a father who overhears his daughter's prayer one night asking for special scarlet ribbons for her hair. This prompts him to search the town for the ribbons, but he returns home empty-handed and brokenhearted because every store is dark and locked. He has tried to answer his daughter's prayer but he is unable to do so. Yet the sentimental ending of the song reveals that the girl wakes up in the morning to find beautiful scarlet ribbons beneath her pillow.

Jesus taught in Matthew 7:7-11 that God wants to give His children "good gifts" if they ask. What loving father gives his son a stone when he asks for bread or a snake if he asks for fish? God's condition is that we ask. James tells us that if we lack wisdom it is up to us to ask for it from God. It is reassuring that God's response is not as we might expect, but is a willingness to give generously and without finding fault (see Jas. 1:5). The father in the ballad tried to answer his daughter's prayer even as the world might try to offer us wisdom when we ask. But God is the only one who can answer our prayer by providing His wisdom.

Sometimes pride seems to be what keeps us from asking. How wasteful it is not to have something because we will not ask for it! God's spiritual wisdom is a need every Christian should acknowledge.

Recognizing that the wisdom the world offers and God's wisdom are different is an important step (see 1 Cor. 2:5,12,13). God is the only source of spiritual wisdom. Sometimes He communicates this wisdom through the Bible; sometimes He plants a thought in our mind as we pray; sometimes His wisdom comes through a growing Christian. (Of course, we need to check every source against the Bible, for God will never contradict Himself.)

The Holy Spirit is our special teacher given by God; in John 14:26 we are reassured that He helps us by teaching us all things and by reminding us of what Christ taught. We are not left alone even in our attempt to apply the wisdom God will generously give.

When was the last time you asked God for His wisdom? Thoughtfully consider the needs in your life that require His help, discernment, and guidance. Ask Him to provide you with spiritual wisdom. Think about the resources He may use to reveal the wisdom to you: the Bible, teachers, friends, prayer, and others.

Read 1 Kings 3:9-14. What could Solomon have asked God for? What did he actually request? What would you ask for if you were given one request that God would answer for you?

List the blessings Solomon received as a result of his sincere, unselfish request.

Day 3 Characteristics of God's Wisdom

At special holiday times in particular, kitchens are filled with sweet, pungent smells of baking and unique edible treats. Each kind of ingredient adds a distinct contribution. Separately, the cinnamon, cloves, nutmeg, nuts, raisins, and sugars are pleasant odors that can make mouths water. When combined with flour and other ingredients, these tastes can become delicious cinnamon rolls that bring out the best of each ingredient.

Concerning wisdom, good and profitable bits and pieces are available to us, but they need to be blended together. They need to contribute to a whole, well-balanced life which demonstrates that the wisdom is practically applied. Even as wonderful as some ingredients smell and taste separately, when combined their value is enhanced and better appreciated. God's wisdom is the same.

The proof that spiritual wisdom has been blended into our life, ingredient by ingredient, is the kind of good life, filled with deeds of humility, described in James 3:13. In verses 17-18 James describes this true wisdom from above which is to become a part of us. James characterizes it as being:

Pure—wisdom's origin is God Himself, and it reflects the purity of His character.

Peaceful—it seeks the gentle ways of decision. The word for peacefulness is used in other places to express ideas of yieldedness, gentleness, and being sweetly reasonable.

Considerate and Submissive—this wisdom represents an openness to reason and a quality of remaining adaptable. It implies a gentle and reasonable attitude.

Full of Mercy—this describes compassion demonstrated through kind actions. It includes forgiveness of others.

Impartial—wisdom is unwavering in its truth. It cannot be shifted back and forth. It remains totally objective and fair.

Sincere—it is straightforward and free from hypocrisy or pretence. It is honest, genuine, and always true.

God's wisdom is characterized by all that is good and positive. Which quality of spiritual wisdom is most attractive to you? Which characteristic is hardest for you to identify in the conflict with the wisdom the world offers? Remember that you can ask God to help you to understand and receive wisdom.

Identify additional characteristics of wisdom listed in Proverbs 8:12-14. What would a person be like who had these traits? Do you know anyone who could be described by these verses?

How much of God's wisdom is revealed in the laws of this country? How about in your own code of ethics?

Day 4 Characteristics of the World's Wisdom

Have you ever had "one of those days"? You know . . . the one that started badly because you overslept. Then, because you were already late, you couldn't spend as much time as you needed to get yourself looking just right. You probably even forgot your coat even though it was raining. It may have been the same day a teacher sprang an unexpected test or assignment on you, and most likely the cafeteria was serving your most dreaded meal for lunch. And of course, since everything else was going wrong, you may have done something almost unforgivably stupid in front of the person you most want to impress. We have all had "those days" or at least the elements of one every now and then.

Just as special ingredients can be combined to make something good to eat, bad characteristics work together to create something undesirable. The world's ideas about wisdom are completely different from God's ideas.

In James 3:14-16, in between descriptions of spiritual wisdom, James explains what kind of wisdom is not inspired by God. He suggests that the world's wisdom includes:

Bitter Jealousy—an attitude of extreme envy.

Selfish Ambition—which produces tension and rivalry. Selfishness demonstrates excessive self-interest and concern.

Disorder—also translated "confusion"—is the opposite of peace.

Every Evil Practice—provides a description of all else that is opposed to spiritual wisdom, everything possible that is contrary to God.

Proverbs 8:13 includes a few more characteristics of the world's wisdom from a different point of view. It says that the Lord's wisdom hates:

Pride and Arrogance—an undue degree of self-importance. This is the ultimate conceit.

Evil Behavior—this broad description refers to action that is depraved and morally bad. It is everything wicked and sin-ful.

Perverse Speech—human words and language which are contrary and opposed to the words of the Lord. Such speech demonstrates outright disobedience to God's laws through blasphemy.

It is easy to observe this kind of wisdom surrounding us in our world. How do you feel personally influenced by what the world tells you is wise? What can you do today to become more aware of God's wisdom in contrast to human wisdom?

Colossians 2:8 shares a warning for Christians. Read it and list what can happen if we are unaware of the contrast between human wisdom and God's wisdom.

What happens at your school that would compare to things on your list? Be especially aware of how Paul's thoughts are applicable to school, government, etc.

Day 5 The Insufficiency of Human Wisdom

Mike Williams was getting madder and madder. He was trying to find a new record shop. It was somewhere downtown, but he was driving around and around without finding it. When he had told his friend Michelle Anderson that he was going to look for it after school, she had said, "It's kind of hard to find, Mike. I was there yesterday for the first time. Want me to draw you a map?"

But Mike had shrugged off the idea that he might need a map. "Just tell me where it is. I'll find it OK," he insisted. Now he wasn't so sure.

Mike thought he could find the new store without any help—doing it his own way. Proverbs has a name for those who think their own way is right: Fools (see Prov. 12:15) and even worse than fools (26:12).

Assuming that they know the right way, the correct answer and the best advice is a way of life for these people. Their outlook is so colored by their personal point of view that they are unable to consider any other perspective. They assume that they know it all. They are usually quite frustrating to be around. They are arrogant—a word that is sometimes defined as "puffed up." That seems an appropriate description, depicting someone trying to be much more than he or she really is. If Mike had not been so sure of his own ability to find the store, he would have accepted the help he needed from Michelle. Instead, he created a problem for himself.

Hannah, rejoicing over finally having a son, offers this advice to those who consider their own knowledge sufficient for every circumstance: "Do not keep talking so proudly or let your mouth speak such arrogance, for the Lord is a God who knows, and by him deeds are weighed" (1 Sam. 2:3).

God also shares His plan for those who consider their own wisdom and thinking superior: "I will put an end to the arrogance of the haughty and will humble the pride of the ruthless" (Isa. 13:11).

Think back over the past week. Have you considered your own wisdom sufficient for solving a problem or planning a course of action? Consider an area of your life that may require acknowledging God's wisdom and perspective; how will you incorporate it into your plan or your solution to a problem?

Read the description of a fool in Proverbs 18:2. How does this describe people you know? How can you avoid being this kind of fool?

Try to recall at least three benefits God offers to those who find pleasure in understanding.

Day 6 Human Understanding and God's Plans

When you travel in an airplane your view of the earth is spectacular. In one glance you can see an area more than a hundred miles around. Distance is compressed so that miles of highway may appear as only a short line.

News stations use airplanes and helicopters to observe the highways so that they can inform motorists about traffic problems or road conditions. A person planning a route while on the ground is limited in his or her ability to choose between the best or quickest options, but a person in an airplane can see the obstacles, hazards and impasses on various roads.

Viewing any situation from an objective point of view creates a more impartial and unprejudiced opportunity for appraisal. Perspective is the key.

In considering wisdom, even in our most sincere efforts we cannot come near to the place of knowing the mind of God. Our human understanding is just not capable of knowing the plans God has for us. Proverbs 19:21 says, "many are the plans in a man's heart, but it is the Lord's purpose that prevails." Proverbs also warns us not to lean on our own understanding (see Prov. 3:5). We must acknowledge that God's ways are higher than our ways and His thoughts higher than our thoughts (see Isa. 55:9).

Even wanting to do what God wants us to do is not enough; we need His guidance. Our efforts must be accompanied by our willingness to accept the fact that we will never completely have God's perspective. We can glimpse parts of it through the Bible and through His ministry in our lives. But because God is infinite and we are merely finite, we will never know as much as He knows or understand as fully as He does. So we must always depend on Him and be thankful for His guidance.

Thoughtfully ask yourself if you have been leaning on your own understanding in doing and planning things this week. How might you need to acknowledge that God's perspective is different from your own? Consider how you can express your thankfulness to God today for His gift of wisdom.

Read Proverbs 16:2. What do people's motives have to do with their plans? Who does it ultimately concern?

What do motives have to do with pursuing wisdom?

D.E.

The Wisdom of Instruction

Day 1: Our Need to Be Taught

Every year Mr. Raney, the woodshop teacher, spends time in the first few class sessions talking about and demonstrating the safety measures that he expects his students to follow. "You've got to protect yourselves," he insists. "I don't want any cut-off fingers or injured eyes in my classes!"

Human beings are self-protective creatures. Our basic biological processes have built-in safety devices. For example, we automatically shut our eyes if something comes toward them. And our bodies are equipped to produce extra antibodies when flu viruses or other enemies invade.

Beyond this natural biological self-preservation, we consciously look out for our own interests. Students who plan to attend college work hard to get good grades in the required college preparatory classes. Those who plan to pursue a trade take classes to learn the necessary skills so they will be able to earn a living. People who plan to live alone for a while learn how to cook. People who plan to drive a car investigate the cheapest gas prices in town and the correct method of checking the oil.

Proverbs tells us that acquiring knowledge and understanding are ways in which we can take care of ourselves. As honey is sweet to the mouth, wisdom is pleasant for the soul (see Prov. 24:13,14). If you find wisdom, "there is a future hope for you, and your hope will not be cut off."

In a positive way God wants us to love ourselves: "He who gets wisdom loves his own soul; he who cherishes understanding prospers" (Prov. 19:8). Other verses in Proverbs say that we are guarded by wisdom; that wisdom is our protector and the way to find favor with God, and that wisdom is our very life (see Prov. 4:6,13; 8:35).

What can we do to gain the instruction that will make us better people? We need to learn so that we can be blessed with the benefits that learning offers us. Proverbs 3:16-18 lists the following things that wisdom can provide for us: long life, riches, honor, pleasant ways, peace, and happiness. Health (and, by implication, hope) are added by Proverbs 15:4 and 4:22.

Incorporating wisdom into our life does require a conscious effort to include it in everything we do. Wisdom must become a part of us, as close as a relative or an intimate friend. The figurative language of Proverbs 7:1-4 suggests that our hearts are tablets on which God's teachings are to be permanently written, and that these teachings need to be bound on our fingers as well. That's like tying a string around your finger to remind yourself of an important matter.

How much of what you are learning is based on God's wisdom and truth? How are you working to incorporate His teaching into your life?

Read David's prayer in Psalm 25:4,5, in which he acknowledges his need to be taught. What does David ask God to teach him? How much time does he allow? How does this compare with the life-styles of many people today?

Day 2 How We Are Taught

On the first day of school, Mrs. Sheldon gave a short quiz to her new freshman students. She said that the quiz would test the students' ability to follow directions. It consisted of a list of about 25 brief instructions regarding things to write on or do with the quiz paper. Mrs. Sheldon told the students that they had only five minutes to read through all of the directions and complete the test. At her signal students proceeded to complete their assignment in one of two ways. Some chose to start right in with the various changes and additions the instructions described, while others first read through the entire quiz. The latter group discovered that the final instruction said to complete only question #1; these students finished in plenty of time and passed the test. Those who "did their own thing" by following each instruction as they read it failed the test.

We often go about learning from God in a similar impatient or inappropriate way. Even if we acknowledge our need to be taught we may not know how to go about learning. God provides the ways we are to learn, and He has special guidelines. Like the students who were responsible for following their teacher's instructions, we are responsible for obeying the directions we receive from God.

In Psalm 119 we are directed to approach God's teaching

(His law, commandments, precepts, and testimonies) in all kinds of ways. The list includes loving, seeking, obeying, considering, pondering, keeping, understanding, meditating on, regarding, believing, hoping in, delighting in, and walking in them. We are to consider God's teaching as being of great value. We are to hide it in our hearts.

Specifically, God teaches us through several sources. **Scripture** is God's written word to us. It can be so useful to us that it can thoroughly equip us for every good work (see 2 Tim. 3:16,17). It also offers us hope (see Rom. 15:4). God has given us **the Holy Spirit** as a helper and teacher of His spiritual truths (see John 14:26). We can rely on Him to enlighten us concerning the Bible and God's will for us. Uniquely, He can teach us even when there is no external teacher available (see 1 John 2:27).

Godly parents are commanded to teach their children (see Deut. 11:19) and are a source of instruction given to us by God. Proverbs 5:7 and 1:8 tell us to listen to them and not to depart from or forsake their words.

In addition, God prepares and uses some **Christians** as teachers of others. Teaching can be a specific gift He delegates to some to be used for His service (see Eph. 4:11,12). Older Christians are admonished to teach younger ones (see Titus 2:3-8).

From whom do you receive most of your teaching? Do your teachers give instruction that provides God's truth and hope? Do you attempt to sincerely follow their instructions as completely as possible?

Consider what Paul says in Philippians 4:9. Paul isn't being conceited; instead he establishes himself as an example for others. What things have you been taught that you need to put into practice?

How does Matthew 28:19,20 apply to Christians you know? If you have been taught from God, what can you teach others?

Day 3 Being Open to God's Teaching

A person who wants to be an outstanding athlete must pursue the goal with wholeheartedness and sacrificial effort. Athletes train, prepare, practice, and compete over and over in an attempt to become progressively better and eventually the best. Most will acknowledge that the drive toward accomplishing their goal is as much mental as physical. They make a decision to compete in order to achieve excellence. In the New Testament, Paul describes a race he is running. It is toward the goal God has called him to and it requires every ounce of strength he has. He realizes that the effort requires "reaching forward"—*if* he presses on, *then* he will lay hold of God's plan for him. *If* an athlete trains well enough, *then* he may win the prize.

We discover in Proverbs that *if* we are open to God's teaching, *then* we will receive His special reward. Proverbs 2:1-22 shares a recipe for a life most Christians would desire. It is an example of a cause and effect that can be incorporated into our lives as we pursue instruction and wisdom.

If we:
- accept (a father's) words (v. 1)
- store up his commands within us (v. 1)
- turn our ear to wisdom (v. 2)
- apply our heart to understanding (v. 2)
- call out for insight (v. 3)
- cry aloud for understanding (v. 3)
- look for it as for silver (v. 4)
- search for it as for hidden treasure (v. 4).

Then we will:
- understand the fear of the Lord (v. 5)
- find the knowledge of God (v. 5)
- understand what is right and just and fair (v. 9).

In a review of the entire second chapter of Proverbs it is exciting to discover how many other promises and assurances are made to those who fulfill the conditions required. God is perfectly faithful; *if* we do our part, *then* He can do His.

The Lord promised David that He would instruct and teach him in the way he should go, with His eye upon him (see Ps. 32:8). The choice was David's to accept or reject the teaching offered. Yet God compares those who refuse instruction to horses or mules who need to be controlled by bits and bridles (see v. 9).

What would you like God to teach you? Identify at least one area in which you would like His direction today; make it your sincere prayer this week. Allow God to teach you with His eye upon you.

Read Proverbs 3:13-15. The benefits of gaining wisdom are described as being more profitable and precious than what? What can be compared with wisdom's value?

What does our society consider more valuable than wisdom? Does God agree?

Day 4 Being Open to Correction

While driving down a busy and dangerous highway, a drunk driver attempted to pass another car even though he could not see the oncoming traffic well. He made a bad judgment and as a result had a head-on collision with a car that was coming from the opposite direction. After the accident the erring driver's record was investigated. He had been ticketed for drunk driving on previous occasions, making the consequences of this action a suspended license. The man had been disciplined by the country's law in one way or another before but had failed to change his practices. He demonstrated his rebellion against the correction given him by deciding to drive again while drunk. In this situation, two people who were injured in the accident were to be forever influenced by his irresponsible decision.

The idea of being open to and accepting correction and discipline is not a popular subject, yet Proverbs recognizes it as being extremely important. The book describes the unfortunate and extremely frustrating result of not heeding correction. To disregard correction identifies a person as a fool, according to Proverbs 15:5, and Webster defines a fool as one who is greatly deficient in good judgment and common sense.

On the other hand, Proverbs 15:32 says that although the one who ignores discipline despises himself, the one who heeds correction gains understanding. By accepting discipline and correction we take care of ourselves; we acknowledge that we do need continual teaching and are willing to make considerations that will make us more wise. Other Proverbs add that those who rebuke or reprove a wise person will not face his hatred but rather his love, and that a rebuke will make a deep impression on a person with understanding and discernment.

It is inevitable that at times God needs to correct us, for no one lives a perfect life. When we acknowledge correction, Proverbs says, we will be honored (see 13:18). Parents discipline their children because of their love and concern for what is best for the child. Discipline is often a demonstration of the parent's interest in the children's character development and desire for them to become godly men and women. Similarly, God proves His love for us by disciplining us (see Prov. 3:11,12). He cares intimately about the kind of people we are; He is interested in what He knows is best for us.

It is possible to reject correction or at least not take it seriously—to the point where our neglect can influence and affect our lives. How might you have ignored God's discipline lately?

Read Proverbs 1:23-33. God wants us to be wise; in order to achieve that goal we are instructed to acknowledge His reproof and counsel. What will happen as a result of not heeding them?

List the characteristics and attitudes of people who refuse to listen to wisdom. How many people at your school act similarly?

Day 5 Being Open to Advice

A young athlete named David Sims was just beginning his professional football career with the Seattle Seahawks when he learned that he had a poorly protected spinal cord. It was a condition not recognized until it caused him some problems during play. Once it was diagnosed, the doctors warned him that he might be paralyzed if he was hit wrong again while playing football. David had to make an important yet very difficult decision: he could heed the doctors' advice or he could risk paralysis in order to pursue a promising opportunity. He chose to give up football.

We all face situations involving choices, and we must decide whether or not to listen to and consider what others tell us. Sometimes the advice offered us is based on personal bias or even selfishness, but often we can invite educated, practical, wise counsel that gives our decision-making process a helpful advantage. The problem is that we often don't seek the advice that could be beneficial to us.

Proverbs has much to say about the role of advice in our plans, and everything it says indicates that this is a vital ingredient. More than that, the book describes how advice and counsel play an important role in the success of our lives.

"Advisors make victory sure" (Prov. 11:14). Even as pursuing instruction demonstrates an interest in insuring our own well-being, so getting counsel increases and further assures that our life will be secure.

However, listening to advice and objectively accepting it can be two different positions. Have you ever shared something with someone who didn't really "hear" you—who listened to your voice but never understood your thought? Have you ever done the same thing to someone else? Listening to sincere and wise advice requires a willingness on our part to be open to its thought and intent, even if we don't agree with it all the time. If David Sims had not understood his doctors' recommendations as helpful counsel, he could have regarded the physicians as well-meaning but misguided people who did not understand his situation.

Proverbs encourages us that we will benefit when we listen to advice. Accepting counsel distinguishes the fool from the one who is wise (see Prov. 12:15). Listening to advice can help us become wise people. Proverbs 19:20 says, " . . . and in the end you will be wise." Gaining wisdom can be a continual process.

Can you remember a time during the last month when someone's counsel made a difference in your decision-making? How often do you sincerely listen to another's advice, weighing his or her opinion and thoughts objectively?

Recall recent plans that have turned out differently than you expected. Read Proverbs 15:22. Could any of the circumstances have been caused by a lack of wise counsel from others?

Make a list of people you respect and could ask advice from in future decision-making and planning. Consider their trustworthiness, honesty, and wisdom; don't overlook friends who have sensible minds and common sense.

Day 6 Remaining Teachable

Young children often wish to be "grown up." They want to be adults because they think adults get to do whatever they want. Being grown up is synonymous with complete freedom. Children don't realize that adults' freedom is accompanied by comparable responsibility. Even if they were aware of the responsibility, they would probably disregard its possible restrictions. Growing up, learning how to accept responsibilities and handle freedom appropriately, is a lifelong process. Becoming mature requires steadfastness, persistence, and a large measure of patience. The word "mature" implies "complete." Almost everyone can become more complete or mature.

Gaining wisdom and learning are lifelong processes as well. Being "grown up" is often not what children expect it to be. But acquiring wisdom and instruction is worth much more than we expect. Almost all of our emotions tend to be contagious. Discontent seems to breed discontent, worry more worry, and joy more joy. Proverbs says that if you instruct a wise man he will grow wiser still, and he who walks with the wise grows wise (see Prov. 9:9; 13:20). In addition, those who are wise "store up knowledge," according to Proverbs 10:14. These Scriptures describe an accumulation which involves gradual yet deliberate building of the instruction and learning offered by God.

If wisdom is to be continually built upon itself then it needs to be an intimate part of us that we value. We are to "buy truth" and are "not to sell it; get wisdom, discipline and understanding" (see Prov. 23:23). People guard and protect the things that mean the most to them. It is to our benefit to accumulate instruction so that we can apply it to our lives in practical ways.

Proverbs instructs parents to "train up a child in the way he should go, even when he is old he will not depart from it"

(22:6). This describes a process that begins in childhood and continues through life. Are you more wise today than you were last year? How do you work at acquiring learning from God?

Read Proverbs 6:6-8. Study the life of the ant described. Is his a short or long-term project? How long do you think his preparation will sustain him?

If the ant were accumulating wisdom, he would gain it steadily, little by little. What kind of example is he for us? Who do you know that is like that?

S.H.

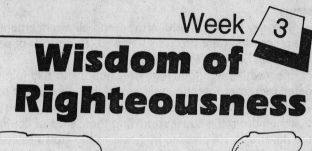

Wisdom of Righteousness

Day 1 The Great Give-Away

The story is told of a multimillionaire who owned nearly the entire city in which he lived. One day the man died of a heart attack, and the population mourned his loss. When his will was read, the man's relatives discovered that he had some unusual instructions for his own funeral. The man requested that his body be dressed in his most expensive suit and propped upright in the back seat of his solid gold Cadillac convertible. The Cadillac was to be chauffeur-driven down Main Street to the cemetery while flowers were strewn on the highway and marching bands played the millionaire's favorite songs.

The day for the funeral arrived and all arrangements for the procession were precisely followed. Thousands of people lined Main Street to see the event.

Meanwhile, a raggedy-looking hobo who had just wandered into town saw the huge crowd and drew closer to see what was going on. He watched amazed as young girls marched down the street sprinkling thousands of flowers on the pavement. He pressed in closer to the crowd to see and hear the bands play the most beautiful music he had ever heard.

Then he saw the Cadillac approaching. His eyes bulged with disbelief as he watched the sparkling limousine pass with the millionaire's corpse propped majestically in the back seat. The hobo was so overcome with awe that he could contain his silence no longer. He shouted out excitedly, "Now that's what I call really living!"

Most of the world sees life through the eyes of our ignorant hobo. Success for most people is measured in terms of amassing enough money, properties and possessions to lead a comfortable, hassle-free life. In underdeveloped countries, "really living" might mean the security of having a roof over one's head and at least one full bowl of rice each day. In more affluent western countries, status symbols of success include cars, boats, video outfits, furniture and wardrobes. Unfortunately, Christians seem to find themselves right in the middle of the race to "keep up with the Joneses."

But, like the hobo, many of us don't have the complete picture. Like many guidelines which the world follows, the "grab all you can" plan for success is the opposite of God's guideline for the righteous. Proverbs 21:25,26 puts it this way: "The sluggard's craving will be the death of him, because his hands refuse to work. All day long he craves for more, but the righteous give without sparing."

While the popular approach to success seems to say "gather what you want" the wisdom of righteousness dictates that we "give what we have." "Better a little with righteousness," another Proverb states, "than much gain with injustice" (Prov. 16:8). Though the Bible never condemns wealth as such, it clearly opposes those who are greedy for it and applauds those who generously distribute it.

Though not a Christian, Mahatma Gandhi, the hero of India, modeled a detachment from material possessions which would put most of the righteous to shame. As a young, affluent lawyer he determined to cut his living expenses in half by focusing on necessities and eliminating luxuries. As the most influential person in India he could carry all his earthly possessions in one bag!

So for the righteous, success is not scored by how much we've accumulated and saved, but by how much we've distributed and spent in Jesus' name in ministry to others. Now that's what I call *really* living!

Jesus had an encounter with a man who apparently had a problem with his possessions. The incident led to a teaching session with Jesus' disciples on the topic of wealth and godliness. Read about it in Mark 10:17-31.

Summarize what Jesus said about wealth and the believer. If Jesus told you to sell all your possessions, which would be the hardest for you to give up? Why?

Day 2 Walking in the Light

As a teenager in West Berlin, Paul was angry, bitter and disillusioned about life. The meaningless treadmill of day-to-day life frustrated him. The hollow state religion forced upon him from infancy bored him.

After high school graduation Paul spurned college education, saying, "I don't even know what life is all about, let alone how to prepare for a career in it." Instead Paul began to travel throughout Europe looking for some answers to his quest for meaning in life. Every journey ended with the same disillusionment and frustration of his teen years.

Paul turned to drugs and eastern religions in an attempt to fill the void in his life. "The primary value of drugs to me was not the 'high,' but hope of a valid religious experience," Paul admits. "I was desperate to find relief from the aching emptiness inside."

Paul's travels eastward led him and thousands of other "flower children" to India, Turkey and finally Afghanistan. While in a restaurant in Kabul, Paul met some Christian young men from his homeland of Germany. They were part of an evangelism team that had come to Afghanistan to share the good news of Jesus Christ with the thousands upon thousands of disillusioned youths who, like Paul, had escaped to the east in search of substance for their lives.

As the young men talked to him about Christ, a light poured into his soul and Paul knew that his long search was over. He embraced Jesus Christ as his Saviour and attached himself to the evangelistic team, drinking in their teaching and encouragement and saturating himself with the Word and Spirit of God.

Soon Paul was sharing his new-found faith with others. The Lord led him back to Berlin and then to Holland where he served with the outreach team. There he married Mary, one of the members of the team which had found him in Kabul.

Later Paul and Mary traveled to the United States where Paul enrolled in Fuller Seminary's School of Missions. Today Paul and Mary work for a Christian research corporation serving a variety of missions organizations by providing statistical data for target groups around the world.

Paul's story clearly illustrates some wise words about guidance found in Proverbs 4:18,19: "The path of the righteous is like the first gleam of dawn, shining ever brighter till the full light of day. But the way of the wicked is like deep darkness; they do not know what makes them stumble."

Without Christ, Paul stumbled in the deep darkness of the emptiness of life. He had about as much hope of finding a meaningful path for his life as would a blindfolded person wandering through a thick forest in the middle of a moonless night! The path does exist, but there is no hope of finding it unless somebody turns on the light.

But for Paul and those who, like him, have discovered the light of life in Jesus Christ, the blindfolds have come off and the light has dawned. Miraculously light appeared on the pathway and we have discovered which way to go. Though we rarely see very far ahead on the pathway, our commitment to develop as "righteous" followers of Jesus Christ seems to increase the candle power which He shines on our way. As the light grows, so does the confidence that we are headed in the right direction.

One of the rules of safe night driving states: "Never drive faster than your headlights will allow you to safely maneuver." Headlight beams extend only so far. Drivers need to make sure they are able to stop or turn safely when the headlights reveal an obstruction in the highway.

Don't worry if you cannot see more than a few days, weeks or months down the path on which God is leading you. The important thing is maneuvering obediently on the stretch of highway you can see right now. The rest of the path will take care of itself.

Read John 1:1-5. What do you think the phrase "that life was the light of men" means? How much of your personal life's path is still yet to be illuminated to you (schooling, career, mate, etc.)? How do you feel about being "in the dark" on some things in your future?

Day 3 He's Only a Prayer Away

"Incoming rockets!" cried the first sergeant as two explosions a half-second apart shattered the predawn stillness, spraying rocks and shrapnel across the camp.

"Cover up! Cover up!" the lieutenant shouted hoarsely. He crouched and waved the startled soldiers toward the bunkers. Two more rockets hit inside the camp, then a third exploded directly in front of two men running for the bunker. They were dead before their bodies hit the ground. Three more were cut down in mid-stride by flying, white-hot shrapnel.

One young private dived into a sand-bagged bunker just as another rocket hit nearby, sending a shower of sparks and shrapnel in every direction. Two other men were in the bunker. One had rolled himself into a ball on the ground and covered his head with his arms. He was sobbing hysterically. The other was barely alive, sprawled grotesquely against the sandbags, blood streaming from his nose and mouth.

"Oh, Jesus God!" the young private moaned fearfully as he peered out of the bunker to see rocket after rocket bludgeon the base and send soldier after soldier into eternity. "Oh Jesus, oh God!" the young man cried. "They've found us, God, and they're going to pound us until there's nothin' left." The private's hands were trembling and his voice rasped like two pieces of sandpaper rubbing against each other as he verbalized his prayer. "If you'll just get me out of this alive, God," he pleaded, weeping, "I'll turn my life around, God. I'll give up everything and live for you." Then he fell on his knees and began, "Our Father, which art in heaven . . . "

Someone once said, "There are no atheists in foxholes." The scene described above, though fictitious, has been repeated countless times as fighting men around the world have faced imminent death in battle. Even some of the most hardened, ungodly people, when standing eye to eye with the stark reality of death, have turned to prayer. Others who would only mention the name of God or Jesus in conjunction with swearing will cry out, "Oh God!" in time of fear, tragedy or panic. It seems as though believers and unbelievers alike automatically reach out to God in some way when up against a life-threatening situation.

But how many foxhole prayers actually get through? Is God duty bound to listen and respond to every "Oh God!" or "Jesus please help me!" which is uttered?

Ultimately, God alone can answer those questions. But there are some wise words in Proverbs 15:29 which give us a clue as to the kind of people who *always* get through: "The Lord is far from the wicked but he hears the prayer of the righteous." There it is! It's the righteous whose prayers are heard.

The righteous are the people who do right. A person becomes righteous by doing the right thing about his relationship to God through Jesus Christ. A right relationship to God is centered on receiving Christ personally and committing one's life to him. A right relationship to God continues as believers live in loving obedience for the one to whom they have committed their lives.

King David indicates that even the righteous may lift a prayer which cannot be heard by God: "If I had cherished sin in my heart, the Lord would not have listened" (Ps. 66:18). A person needs not only to establish a relationship with Christ, but to maintain that righteousness through avoiding sin. The Christian who has made a commitment of his or her life, but is living as though he or she had not, runs the risk of praying prayers which bounce off heaven's door unheard.

So wise up, live righteously and watch those answers to prayer roll in!

Read Psalm 34:15-22. List the benefits which the righteous receive in relation to trouble.

Can you think of some personal experiences of tragedy or fear in which you discovered firsthand that the Lord "hears the prayer of the righteous"?

Day 4 See the Righteous Run

The 1929 Rose Bowl game between the University of California and Georgia Tech stands out in college football history because of one bizarre play by one confused player. During a Georgia Tech drive toward the end zone the ball was fumbled. The loose ball was alertly scooped up by Cal's Roy Riegels who tucked the ball into his side and headed toward the end zone—but he was running the wrong way! In the confusion of picking up the ball, Riegels got turned around and mistakenly began running toward his opponent's goal line. Riegels misinterpreted the crowd's horrified screams as cheers of encouragement as he raced toward what he thought would be a Cal touchdown.

One of Riegels's teammates finally caught up with the determined runner and tackled him on Cal's two-yard line. The California Bears punted on the next play but it was blocked by Tech for a safety. Georgia Tech won the game 8-7.

Since then Roy Riegels has been known as "Wrong Way" Riegels. In the passage of time, any good plays which Riegels might have accomplished in his football career have been forgotten. "Wrong Way" Riegels's claim to fame in football history rests on one botched play consuming less than thirty seconds.

Human nature seems to be that way, doesn't it? We tend to forget a string of successes in our lives or the lives of our friends and focus on a mistake, failure or sin. As Christians we sometimes allow unrealistic guilt to engulf us when the successful progress of our lives is momentarily interrupted by "one botched play consuming less than thirty seconds." We're suspicious that the history of our spiritual adventure being written in heaven will somehow begin with the words "Wrong Way" in front of our names.

Two wise Proverbs help provide some needed perspective on the success and failure which is part of our lives. Proverbs

25:26 warns us of the danger of compromise with sin in our lives: "Like a muddled spring or a polluted well is a righteous man who gives way to the wicked." Yes, the impurity which saturates our godless society can seep into the life of the Christian who is not on guard against it. It takes very little foreign matter in a spring or well to render it unfit for human consumption. And let's face it—our chief enemy the devil is continually plotting against us in an attempt to cause us to fail in our commitment to righteousness (see 1 Pet. 5:8).

But Proverbs 11:6 offers an encouraging "other side of the coin" to those who are determined to run with Jesus: "The righteousness of the upright delivers them, but the unfaithful are trapped by evil desires." Sure, there will be times when you will pick up the ball and run the wrong way. But because of your commitment to Christ there will be many more times when you will go the *right* way. Unlike human nature, the divine nature of our Lord allows Him to forgive and forget the wrong-way runs we confess to Him (see 1 John 1:9). In the meantime, the growing list of successful right-way runs is being written in God's record book in indelible ink.

The apostle John offers some insights on the requirements and rewards of practical righteousness, which arises from our relationship of "abiding" with Christ. What do you learn from the following verses on the right-way and wrong-way runs of the righteous? John 15:5-8; John 15:16,17; 1 John 2:1-6.

Day 5 Safety in Stormy Weather

There is a joke going around about a preacher trapped in his home by the rising floodwaters of a vicious hurricane. The preacher was standing patiently in the doorway of his home with the flood swirling around his waist when a rescue rowboat steered close. "We're here to save you, preacher," called the rescuers. "Climb in!"

"I'm not climbing in your boat," the preacher called back, "because I'm trusting God." After pleading unsuccessfully with the preacher for several minutes, the rescuers rowed off to seek other victims.

About an hour later the flood had risen several more feet and the preacher was hanging out his second story window as another rescue boat motored near to save him. "I'm not climbing in your boat because I'm trusting God," the preacher insisted piously. So the second boat roared away to help others in need.

Soon the floodwaters had driven the preacher to his last perch of safety—the chimney of his house. A rescue helicopter spotted him and hovered low, calling for him to grab hold of the rope ladder which they had extended to him. "I'm not getting on your helicopter," the preacher shouted above the engine's roar, "because I'm trusting God." Again the preacher refused additional invitations to be rescued and the helicopter flew away.

Shortly the preacher marched fuming through the pearly gates of heaven and angrily approached the Lord. "What's the big idea?" the preacher sputtered. "I trusted you to rescue me and you never showed up!"

"I don't know why you're angry at me," the Lord replied calmly. "I sent you two boats and a helicopter."

On the serious side, there are few things as devastating in our world as a flood. We've all seen news film showing relentless floodwaters uprooting giant trees, pushing homes off their foundations and carrying away anything which was not securely anchored.

The Bible often refers to the trials and troubles of life as a storm. Sometimes the pressures of getting through school and the problems of getting along with our parents and peers seem to sweep around us like the waters of a flood. And, like the floodwaters testing the durability of even the most securely rooted structures, the storms of our lives cause us to wonder sometimes how well we will hold up under the pressure.

Again the wisdom of the Proverbs comes to our rescue and gets us in touch with our roots. One Proverb describes the security of the righteous *in the midst* of life's storms: "The righteous will never be uprooted, but the wicked will not remain in the land" (Prov. 10:30). Another Proverb gives the happy report *at the end* of each storm: "When the storm has swept by, the wicked are gone, but the righteous stand firm forever" (Prov. 10:25).

We are assured that the righteous—those who have committed their lives to Christ and commit every day to living out that right relationship to Him—will weather the storms. Even though we are not immune to the pounding of the storm, we've got the immoveable Rock of Ages to hang onto.

What storms are currently threatening to uproot you?

Proverbs 18:10 says, "The name of the Lord is a strong tower; the righteous run into it and are safe." What are some practical ways you can "run into" the safety of the "strong tower"?

Day 6 Singing in the Light

In Walt Disney's animated version of "The Legend of Sleepy Hollow," Ichabod Crane, the gangly, timid teacher, is terrified by rumors of the headless horseman who allegedly haunts the hollow. In the closing scenes, Ichabod reluctantly mounts his scraggly-looking horse to ride home through the night-darkened forest.

As his horse plods sleepily through the darkness, Ichabod peers nervously around every corner in fear that the headless horseman, whose legend had been reviewed to Ichabod's hor- ror at that evening's party, might be stalking him.

In an attempt to quiet his fears and convince himself that he is not in danger, Ichabod begins whistling in the dark. Though his heart is pounding in terror, he attempts to keep his composure by whistling a happy tune.

His greatest fears are realized, of course, when the head- less horseman charges at him out of the night. Both Ichabod and his panic-stricken horse flee Sleepy Hollow in a cloud of dust, never to return.

All of us can identify with Ichabod's whistling-in-the-dark episode. When we are stalked by fear, guilt or sin—real or imagined—we often try to convince ourselves and others that everything is okay by humming a happy tune, hoping that everything will appear all right.

But Proverbs 29:6 makes a distinction for us between whistling in the night and singing in the light: "An evil man is snared by his own sin, but a righteous one can sing and be glad." The Ichabod-type whistling in the dark is an outward attempt to quiet fears and soothe guilt. But the singing that Proverbs 29:6 is talking about is the music that only the righ- teous know about—those who have established a right rela- tionship with God through His Son Jesus and who maintain that relationship through right living.

Furthermore, whistling in the dark—trying to convince ourselves and others that everything is okay when it's not— springs from a guilty or fear-ridden conscience. Our con- science is a God-created early-warning device designed to alert us to danger or sin. Trying to cover up the warning sig- nals of the conscience is like turning off a blaring smoke detector without looking for the fire. We may be able to quiet the warning but the real danger rages on unchecked.

There is a joyful song which wells up inside those who learn to respond to the message of warning God sends through His Spirit and our conscience. It's the song of a clean conscience, one which is washed by quick obedience to the One who makes us righteous.

So you can choose your own kind of music. But why whistle in the night when you can sing in the light?

Several New Testament verses speak of the benefits of a clean conscience. What do you learn about the subject from the following: 1 Timothy 1:5; Titus 1:15,16; Hebrews 9:11-14; 10:22?

E.S.

The Benefits of Wisdom

Day 1 The Value of Wisdom

Brad and Darcy, brother and sister, are having the time of their lives. Their parents have brought them to a small island in the Caribbean for a summer-long vacation. They have enjoyed swimming in the ocean, sunning on the beaches, exploring the exotic sights and sounds.

But now things are getting more exciting than they could imagine. A new friend of theirs, a resident named Jack, is taking them on a treasure hunt. He claims to know where a pirate treasure chest is buried.

The three young people make their way to a remote area of the island, toting shovels and sandwiches. Darcy and Brad can hardly believe that anyone could still find buried treasure, but Jack is confident. At any rate, it's an adventure whether they find anything or not. And just the faint possibility that it might be true creates an excitement that makes the sky seem more blue and the trees more green.

At last the adventurers arrive at their destination. Jack takes them through an elaborate ritual of counting paces from this tree and that rock, following a much-folded and ancient-looking map. When the last segment has been paced off, they take up their shovels and begin to dig. Deeper and deeper goes the hole until "Clunk"—there's something solid! Feverishly they scatter the sandy soil in every direction until they can free the object. Sure enough, it is an old, battered sea chest. With almost unbearable excitement oozing out of every pore, the three young people lift the chest out of the hole, break the lock with a rock, and raise the lid. Before them sparkles an incredible hoard of gold coins, loose diamonds, emeralds, rubies, ropes of pearls. They dig their hands in, shouting and laughing and whooping. "We're rich, we're rich," they yell, over and over again.

Can you identify with the excitement of finding a treasure chest full of valuable jewels? It's enough to make the heart race and the adrenalin pump.

There's a treasure chest that is full of valuables worth far more than earthly silver, gold, rubies and pearls. That treasure chest is the wisdom of God. Read Proverbs 3:13-18 and underline the words that compare wisdom with jewels and precious metals. Then make a list of the benefits to be obtained from wisdom.

Day 2 God Will Take Care of You

Little children argue about which one is Mommy's favorite. Students jockey to be noticed and praised by the teacher. Politicians try to convince the public to vote for them. Presidents go on television to explain to the nation just why they had to take the action that cost the lives of a number of marines. Human beings need the acceptance and favor of other human beings.

But there lies a deeper need behind that one. It is the need for God's favor and acceptance. Some deny the need and therefore do not seek out the ways in which it can be fulfilled. They settle for seeking acceptance on a human level.

Those, however, who acknowledge their need for God and seek Him out find that He responds magnificently. The slightest movement on our part toward Him produces a most generous response from Him.

For example, the writer of Proverbs says, "My son, do not forget my teaching, but keep my commands in your heart . . . . Let love and faithfulness never leave you; bind them around your neck, write them on the tablet of your heart. Then you will win favor and a good name in the sight of God and man" (Prov. 3:1,3,4). As we keep God's teachings—His wisdom—before us, as we concentrate on the words He has given us, He responds by giving us His favor. Proverbs 2 adds to the picture. If people accept His words, search for understanding, and value His wisdom as a great treasure, then "He holds victory in store for the upright, he is a shield to those whose walk is blameless, for he guards the course of the just and protects the way of his faithful ones" (Prov. 2:7,8).

God's favor and protection—what a great benefit of wisdom!

Take some time to learn more about this idea by reading Proverbs 2:1-11 and Proverbs 3:1-6 slowly and carefully. Underline with one color phrases and sentences that tell what you should do, and with another color those that tell what God will do.

Day 3 Understanding and Common Sense

Have you ever thought about how much of life is affected by the need for common sense? Just take a mental stroll through your home. Common sense keeps you from sticking your fingers into the hot burners on the kitchen stove. It keeps you from stabbing your arm to see how sharp the carving knife is. It keeps you from drinking the Drano. It keeps you from jumping out the second-story windows or laying a burning match on the carpet after lighting the fireplace or leaving the front door wide open when you go to bed at night.

On a more positive side, common sense tells you that you need to study if you want good grades; that you need to eat reasonably well if you want to be healthy and enjoy life; that the way to win friends is to be a friendly person.

Common sense flows through life in such an essential way that we sometimes don't even think about it. But the examples in the preceding paragraphs show how necessary it is.

Our heavenly Father has an infinite supply of common sense. In His book He talks to His people about such down-to-earth things as putting a railing around the flat rooftop of a house, so that no one can fall off (see Deut. 22:8). He gives good advice for relationships: "A gentle answer turns away wrath, but a harsh word stirs up anger" (Prov. 15:1).

Not only does God have a great supply of common sense, He also offers understanding, sound judgment, and discernment to those who will seek them out. And He promises to those who do, "Then you will go your way in safety, and your foot will not stumble; when you lie down, you will not be afraid; when you lie down, your sleep will be sweet. Have no fear of sudden disaster or of the ruin that overtakes the wicked, for the Lord will be your confidence and will keep your foot from being snared" (Prov. 3:23-26).

As you go about your regular activities for the next few days, pay special attention to the ways common sense operates in your life. And watch particularly for ways in which God's kind of wisdom can make your life better.

Day 4 Living the Right Way

Why does God care about people living the right way—that is, according to standards that He Himself has set? Is it because He is an old killjoy, a curmudgeon who loves rules for the sake of rules and who can't stand to see people enjoying themselves?

Far from it! He is a loving Father who wants the best for His children. Because He made us and the world we live in, He's the best authority on what will truly make us happy. That's why He says in His Word, "Trust in the Lord with all your heart, and lean not on your own understanding; in all your ways acknowledge him, and he will make your paths straight" (Prov. 3:5,6). Following His wisdom will lead to a life full of light and joy.

What, then, does following His wisdom entail? Proverbs gives a couple of examples in chapter 2. For one thing, "Wisdom will save you from the ways of wicked men, from men whose words are perverse, who leave the straight paths to walk in dark ways, who delight in doing wrong and rejoice in the perverseness of evil, whose paths are crooked and who are devious in their ways" (vv. 12-15). People today, just as in Bible times, are subjected to many pressures from the people around them. A classmate asks you to hold your test paper on your desk in a way that will permit her to copy your answers. A friend who is dating an older guy against her parents' orders tells them she's going to your house when she is actually going out with her friend. She asks you to cover for her if her parents call. What do you do in cases like this? The world's wisdom might suggest that you cooperate in order to help out your friends and maintain the relationships.

But God's wisdom can help you see that it's folly to dabble in the ways of darkness, no matter how mild the actions might seem.

Another area is the abuse of God's glorious gift of sexuality. Proverbs 2:16-19 describes the folly of getting involved with adultery. Many other Scriptures speak of God's desire that sex be reserved for marriage. (See, for example, 1 Cor. 6:12-20; Col. 3:5; 1 Thess. 4:3; Heb. 13:4.) God didn't give us this rule because He doesn't like sex (after all, He created it!) but because He likes it so much, and loves us so much, that He wants our experience of sex and marriage to be the most wonderful experience possible. And that can happen only if we do it His way. Now it's true that being married doesn't automatically guarantee great sex, and being unmarried doesn't automatically guarantee rotten sex, but the long-term effects are what count. And in the long run, a marriage between Spirit-filled Christians who are intimate spiritually, emotionally and physically just can't be beat. It's worth waiting for!

Day 5 Sweeter Than Honey

Snack time! Fix yourself a little treat! Take your favorite bread, add a layer of creamy yellow butter, then top it off with a generous spread of golden honey. Delicious!

Now, as you savor the taste of the honey, consider this: "Eat honey, my son, for it is good; honey from the comb is sweet to your taste. Know also that wisdom is sweet to your soul; if you find it, there is a future hope for you, and your hope will not be cut off" (Prov. 24:13,14). The wisdom God offers is compared to the sweetness of honey; and God's Word promises that finding His wisdom will give you hope.

The New Testament has a lot to say about hope. For example: "Praise be to the God and Father of our Lord Jesus Christ! In his great mercy he has given us new birth into a living hope through the resurrection of Jesus Christ from the dead, and into an inheritance that can never perish, spoil or fade—kept in heaven for you, who through faith are shielded by God's power until the coming of the salvation that is ready to be revealed in the last time" (1 Pet. 1:3-5). Our hope rests on Christ and His resurrection—what a great foundation! And with that hope we also have an inheritance waiting for us.

Imagine all the money ever accumulated by a Getty or a Rockefeller or an Onassis. Imagine all the art treasures, all the fabulous jewel collections, all the valuable cars and airplanes of the world gathered together in one place. It would be an impressive pile of wealth for someone to inherit! But our inheritance in Christ is infinitely more valuable, because it is eternal life (see Titus 1:2).

Another fascinating facet of our future hope is found in 1 John: "How great is the love the Father has lavished on us, that we should be called children of God! And that is what we are! The reason the world does not know us is that it did not know him. Dear friends, now we are children of God, and what we will be has not yet been made known. But we know that when he appears, we shall be like him, for we shall see him as he is. Everyone who has this hope in him purifies himself, just as he is pure" (3:1-3).

Three points stand out in the section just quoted: (1) The love of God. All the talk about His wisdom and right living and doing things His way springs from His love, which seeks the best for His children. (2) We shall see Him as He is. In this life we do not see Jesus in the flesh. We can't touch God's hand physically. Even our perception of the Lord's character and attributes is filtered through our fallen human ability to reason and understand. But one day the filter will disappear and we will know Him without barriers. (3) We shall be like Him! The love, the light, the joy and all the other things that attract people to Jesus will be fully developed in us too. That's something to look forward to! You might want to spend some time thanking God for these benefits.

Day 6 A Good Night's Sleep

Have you ever spent a night tossing and turning in bed, worrying about tomorrow's exam or about the repercussions of an argument you had with your best friend?

Did you know that one of the benefits of living by God's wisdom is sleeping well? Take a look at Proverbs 3:21,24: "My son, preserve sound judgment and discernment, do not let them out of your sight . . . . When you lie down, you will not be afraid; when you lie down, your sleep will be sweet."

A good night's sleep is just one part of the physical well-being and prosperity that can result from doing things God's way. While it's true that wonderful, obedient, Spirit-filled Christians sometimes get cancer or suffer from other illnesses, or lose their jobs and run out of money, the basic principle still remains. If you do things God's way, generally you'll be a lot better off.

The writer of Proverbs (who, by the way, addressed his thoughts to his son; women need not feel excluded by this) said, "My son, do not forget my teaching, but keep my commands in your heart, for they will prolong your life many years and bring you prosperity" (Prov. 3:1,2). If you live by God's book, you will tend to stay away from harmful habits like gluttony and getting involved in the immoral and criminal activities of acquaintances. That in itself should tend to prolong your life and preserve your resources for doing useful things.

For example, "Honor the Lord with your wealth . . . then your barns will be filled to overflowing, and your vats will brim over with new wine" (Prov. 3:9,10). You probably don't have barns full of crops or vats full of wine, but you get the idea. Put God first in your life and you will reap the benefits. For Christians these benefits may tend to be spiritual as often as or more often than they are material. The hope we discussed last time, the confidence of knowing we will be with Christ throughout eternity, the blessings He gives here and now—for many, these are more valuable than all the barns and crops and vineyards in the world. And they are available to us right now.

Here are some more Scriptures about the physical well-being and prosperity that result from following God's wisdom. Look them up, read them, think about how they apply to your life today: Proverbs 14:30; Proverbs 1:33; Proverbs 28:26.

C.B.

Wisdom with Humility

Day 1: Who Is the Truly Humble Person?

"It is better to be of a humble spirit with the lowly, than to divide the spoil with the proud." (Proverbs 16:19)

"My name is Norman Snerdly."
"My name is Norman Snerdly."
"My name is Norman Snerdly."
Remember that old game show, "To Tell the Truth"? Three contestants would come out, all claiming to be Norman Snerdly (or some other person). But only one was telling the

truth. The others were imposters.

Three persons described below all claim to be humble people. Can you pick the one who doesn't lie?

Contestant number one is a very rich and powerful man. He's shy, so he tends to let others walk on him. Often he'll stand in a group of talkers, just listening. He doesn't join in because he's bashful.

Contestant number two is also a very rich and powerful man. He's friendly and outgoing, and kind to everyone. He often acts as if being wealthy and strong doesn't really mean all that much to him.

Contestant number three is a poor man. He hasn't any money, he dresses shabbily, and he has no power in this world. People often don't know he's around.

Made up your mind? Well, you've probably guessed it's not contestant number one. He's shy and bashful, not humble. And it's not contestant number three. He's not humble, he's just poor! (You can be both poor and humble, but nothing in the description of number three indicates active humility.)

Contestant number two is our man. He is a rich and powerful man, yet he doesn't take that into account in his friendship with those around him. That's humility!

You see, Christians too are very rich and powerful people. We are children and heirs of the King of Everything. Yet we are admonished over and over again in the Bible, as we shall see in this series of devotions, to be humble in both attitudes and actions. We are to be the lowest of the lowly and the servants of others.

But in a world of greed and ambition, of celebrity worship and "me first" thinking, is it really "better to be of a humble spirit with the lowly, than to divide the spoil with the proud"? What is humility, and why is it wise to be humble?

To answer these questions, let's start first with one of the all-time classic examples of humanity's arrogance and puffed up self-importance, a monument to monumental pride; the tower of Babel.

Read Genesis 11:1-9.

1. Who were the principal characters involved in this incident?

2. What three things did mankind propose to do? (See verses 3 and 4.)

3. What was the method used to try to reach heaven?

4. What attitudes or reasons are displayed in mankind's aborted attempt to reach into heaven?

5. What was the result? Why did it happen that way?

Keep in mind that ancient pyramids and temples like the tower of Babel were often an attempt to reach God (or gods) in an effort either to dethrone Him, or to receive unmerited gifts and blessing from Him.

In our modern age we'd scoff at this. Yet how many people—even Christians—treat God as if He is some kind of Santa Claus? A God who is there only to bless our own wills, rather than a God who wants us to conform our wills to His.

Attempting to make God bend His will to ours is an incredible act of pride. In tomorrow's devotion we will read a story that has a couple of parallels with the tower of Babel incident, but is a striking example of humility.

Day 2: A Step Toward Humility

"When pride comes, then comes dishonor, but with the humble is wisdom." (Proverbs 11:2, *NASB*).

Read Luke 19:1-10, then answer these brain benders:

1. Who were the principal characters involved in this incident?

2. The people we studied yesterday tried to build a tower to reach God. What did Zacchaeus do to try to reach Jesus?

3. Why, do you suppose, was Zacchaeus trying to see Jesus? How does his motive differ from the motives of the Babel tower builders?

4. What were the results (vv. 5-10)?

Zacchaeus was a rotten little creep. Because he was a chief tax collector in a day when tax collectors could use any means, even violence, to collect money, he was unquestionably an unethical, much-hated man. The Jews would have considered him a traitor to Israel, since he collected taxes for the Roman conquerors.

But something stirred in Zacchaeus's heart. He sensed a need to see Jesus. He was spiritually starving, and somehow he knew that Jesus Christ held the full dinner plate. Zacchaeus climbed the tree.

Jesus told him to come down and make room for Him at his house. The crowd grumbled, saying that Jesus was going to be the guest of a sinner. Oh, how wrong they were!

You see, Jesus was not and never is anyone's guest. He is the Lord. He *told* Zacchaeus to make room for Him—He didn't *ask*. Zacchaeus obeyed. And as we learn in verses 8 and 9, Zacchaeus repented of his evil deeds and gained salvation.

Did you notice the difference between Zacchaeus's motivation in climbing that tree and mankind's motivation in climbing the tower? Zacchaeus simply wanted to see Jesus, and as a result he became a saved believer, a "son of Abraham." Not so those who built the tower of Babel. They hoped to push God aside.

Here are two very important points you must always keep in mind:

1. Mankind's goal in life, as typified by the tower of Babel story, is to achieve; to do. They said, "Let us build a city and a tower. Let us make a name for ourselves" (see Gen. 11:4). But God's goal, as we see in the story of Zacchaeus, is much different. He doesn't care nearly as much about what we can *do*

as about what we can *be*. Jesus said, "he, too, is a son of Abra-ham." Zacchaeus was lost, but Jesus found and saved him.

Today, humanity's goal seems to be doing things like making money, achieving success, gaining power. None of these things are necessarily wrong, but they fall far short of God's goal for mankind. His goal is what we can actually be: loving, forgiving, kind, faithful; and so on. (See Gal. 5:22,23.) That's what God cares about. What do you care about?

2. The builders of the tower of Babel were attempting to maintain their unity as a people (see Gen. 11:4). But their deed led to the very scattering that they had wanted to avoid. Zacchaeus's humble act of repentance (see Luke 19:8) led to salvation.

And that is the first act of true humility: repentance. To repent, in the Christian sense, means to turn away from the old life of sin and pride, to a new life committed to the Lord and Saviour. If you have never repented and turned your life over to the lordship of Jesus Christ, and if you have no inten-tion of doing so, you may as well forget about the rest of this chapter. We can teach you nothing about the wisdom of humility!

Day 3: Are You Content with Yourself or with Christ?

"The Lord will tear down the house of the proud" (Prov-erbs 15:25, *NASB*).

On Day One of this chapter, we studied the tower of Babel story and learned about humanity's pride of achievement apart from God. Day Two showed us the first step of true humility: repentance. Today we'll study the interesting con-trast between the pride of self-contentment (being satisfied with life apart from Christ) and the humility of giving one's life completely to Christ (being Christ-content).

Read Philippians 3:1-6. In verse 3, Paul tells us that we are the "true circumcision," which is his way of saying we are the true believers as opposed to the false troublemakers mentioned in verse 2. Paul also points out that we are not to put "confidence in the flesh," meaning that there is no way we can possibly be good enough to reach heaven on our own apart from God.

But then, with tongue in cheek, Paul describes how he, more than anyone, could put confidence in his own goodness if it were possible to do so (see vv. 4-6).

1. List the seven things that set Paul above the crowd. Tell why each one would have been so important in the eyes of a religious Jew in those days.

2. Name some things that you or others today might proudly and mistakenly think God would be impressed with. Take some time with this one.

3. Read the first half of Proverbs 15:25 and tell how it relates to Paul's pretended arrogance.

Now read Philippians 3:7-11.

4. In verse 7, what things does Paul count as loss?

5. In verse 8, what things does Paul count as loss? Why?

6. In verse 9 Paul says that righteousness does not come from the Old Testament law, but from what?

So what do we learn about pride and humility from this entire passage? We see that Paul, before he became a Christian, put a great deal of effort into being righteous and blameless before God. He didn't need to trust God for the gracious gift of salvation. He could earn it on his own! We see this same sort of arrogance in people who think they can earn a trip to heaven by being "good" or by being religious. (Remember the "false circumcision" in verse 2?)

After Paul became a Christian, he realized that everything he had done to earn God's favor was a washout. Instead, Paul learned the humility of trusting God by faith and allowing

Jesus to be absolute Lord of his life (see v. 8). Instead of placing his trust in himself—being self-content apart from God— he placed his trust in Christ. He lived the humility of giving his life totally to Jesus. He was Christ-content.

For your "homework assignment," think of some ways you could humbly trust God today, rather than trusting your own abilities.

Day 4: Staying by God's Side

"The reward of humility . . . [is] riches, honor, and life" (Proverbs 22:4, *NASB*).

An extremely fat woman—is rotund a nicer word?— caught my eye. But it wasn't her proportions that made me torque my neck as I looked again. It was the two little boys with her.

My parents and I had gone to the zoo to see the animals. I was just a little kid at the time and was fascinated by the apes, snakes, and trained seals. But it's that woman and her two children that I still remember to this day. Why? Because she had tied ropes around their necks and was leading them around like two dogs on chains!

Perhaps I should say that the boys were leading her, for they were straining with all their might at the end of their leashes, trying to see the apes, snakes, and trained seals. But, alas for them, mom outweighed them by a large margin.

There's a spiritual lesson to be learned from this, and we'll get to it after you read Micah 6:6-8 and answer the following questions.

1. List five things mentioned in verses 6 and 7 that someone might bring to the Lord in an attempt to make right his or her sins.

2. From what you've learned so far in this series of devotions, why are the things listed in verses 6 and 7 futile and fruitless?

3. What are the three things God requires in verse 8?

Let's focus in on the phrase, "to walk humbly with your God" (as it reads in the *NASB* version). Walking humbly with God means to love Him, to obey His words, to give Him complete control. It means to stay by His side.

Those two little boys weren't staying by their mom's side. They were stretching those ropes to the limit. That's why she had them tied to her.

We Christians are often guilty of trying to lead the way, to do what we want to do, to stay out at the end of our leash away from God and close to the apes, snakes, trained seals and other things of this world that fascinate us.

Don't do that. Instead, remember Proverbs 22:4. It promises that God will supply everything if we remain humble.

Day 5: Practicing Our Humility

"The fear of the Lord is the instruction for wisdom, and before honor comes humility" (Proverbs 15:33, *NASB).*

To this point, we've learned several important things about humility:

• Though we Christians are royalty, the children of Almighty God, we are to walk humbly, in both attitudes and actions.

• God is not concerned about what we can achieve in our lifetime as much as with what we can become: loving, kind, and so forth.

• The first step of Christian humility is repentance.

• No amount of effort to be holy and righteous will pay off.

Instead, we are to humbly submit to the lordship of Jesus Christ.

• We are to walk humbly at God's side. If we do so, He will reward us.

Assuming we wish to apply all of this to our own lives, let's talk about some specific acts of humility that we can immediately begin to practice.

Read John 13:1-17.

1. What did Jesus do in verse 5?

2. Why did Peter object, and what was Christ's response? (See vv. 6-10.)

3. What principle of humility do you see in verses 12-15? Who is our example of humility?

4. What promise does Christ make to those wise people who humbly serve others? (See vv. 16,17.)

Read Matthew 20:25-28.

5. What must a Christian do to become great in God's eyes?

6. What did Christ do as an example? (Which we hope we won't have to imitate!)

So we see that one important attitude and action of humility is to be a servant. Even Christ Himself, the glorious Lord of Heaven, "emptied Himself, taking the form of a bondservant . . . He humbled Himself by becoming obedient to the point of death, even death on a cross" (Phil. 2:7,8, *NASB*). Read the next three verses to see what the results of being a humble servant were!

What sort of servant things can we do for each other? Here are some ideas:

• Ask your Bible teacher or youth minister if you can help in any way.

• If you drive, give people rides to church meetings.

• Pray specific prayers for all your friends.

But why am I telling you this? Take the next few minutes to think of as many ways as you can to serve others. For help, read Philippians 2:3,4; Ephesians 5:21; 1 John 4:7; and Romans 12:3-18.

Now go back to that passage in John 13 and notice something about Peter. In verse 8, Peter refused to let Jesus wash his feet. On the surface, it sounds like Peter was being humble. "No, Lord! I'm not worthy that you, the Son of God, should wash my stinking feet!" But actually, it was a supreme act of pride! Can you figure out why? Take a minute to come up with an answer. If you can't, answer is below.

You see, Peter committed the ultimate act of pride: he told Jesus Christ what He should do, or rather what He couldn't do. The arrogance! But how many times have we been guilty of doing the same thing? It might sound humble to say, "God can't do great things with me because I'm so weak or sinful. He can't use me because I haven't been a Christian very long or I don't know the Bible very well." But that's false humility. You're actually using a falsely humble attitude as an excuse to avoid God. God can do whatever He wants to do. Don't tell Him He can't use you! He can and He will, if you'll humbly submit to His rule.

Day 6: How's Your Humility?

"For though the Lord is exalted, yet He regards the lowly; but the haughty He knows from afar" (Psalm 138:6, *NASB*).

We have gone about as far as we can go in our study of humility. We are out of days and out of pages. So now is a perfect time to pull a *pop quiz* on you! Let's see just who's humble and who isn't.

Get out your pencil. Ready? Now turn to Matthew 5:1-12 and follow these instructions:

1. Make a list of all the verses that you feel describe you.

2. Make another list of all the verses you don't qualify for yet.

3. Make a list of any verses you aren't sure about or don't understand.

If list number one is the longest, you have passed the test; you are probably a humble person. All these verses describe traits of humility. Either you're humble, or you're a liar!

If list number two is longest, you need to work on your "humility factor." Start over at Day One and begin applying everything you read!

And if you have a number three list, we've made some comments and noted some verses that may help explain how Matthew 5:1-12 is so intimately related to humility.

Verse three can be taken several ways. For example, Jesus may have meant that those who are spiritually bankrupt are blessed because Christ the Saviour has arrived. But more in line with our study of humility, Jesus may have been saying that people who have nothing in this world that they can depend upon, can depend only upon Almighty God. A humble person never puts his or her trust in anything other than God. Remember Paul in Philippians 3:1-11.

Matthew 5:4 probably refers first and foremost to those downtrodden Jews who were patiently waiting for the Messiah to come. That verse still applies today. Christ, sent from God, comes into the heart of the one who longs to find the truth. Think back to the story of Zacchaeus in Luke 19:1-10.

Matthew 5:5 tells us that the meek, humble, and gentle persons shall inherit the earth. That's the new earth yet to come (see 2 Pet. 3:13).

Matthew 5:6 reminds us of Philippians 3:8-11 and Proverbs 22:4.

Matthew 5:7-12 are self-explanatory, but it might be good to say that verses 7 and 9 speak of outward actions for the benefit of others. That reminds us of the humility of service (see John 13:1-17; Matt. 25–28).

All these passages from the Bible speak of the things that a humble Christian can expect to feel or experience.

In reference to this subject, and to the first page of this chapter, will the real Norman Snerdly please stand up?

T.F.

Week 6

Wisdom with Time

Day 1 Our Days are Numbered

Some day a space ship may hurtle from this small planet at the speed of light. The young pilot, braced for a five-year voyage with ample supply of food and entertainment, sits in sorrow at his controls. Soft tears run down his cheeks. Quiet sobs break the sound of whirling machinery.

His grief is for a mother and father he will never see again, for a fishing buddy who will be represented only by a moss-covered marker when the pilot returns. For when the pilot and his crew come back from their historic adventure they will be the only ones of their generation alive on earth. All of the others will have been dead for hundreds of years. The spacecraft crew will have aged only five years, the relative length of their trip. They will have a new world to adjust to and perhaps a new culture and language to learn.

A science fiction fantasy? Perhaps, but many scientists agree that the scenario just described could happen today if we had the technology to travel at the speed of light. It is part of Einstein's theory. Somehow at the speed of light time is warped for the traveler (although it appears normal to him) while the rest of us age at a rate that is normal for us.

Time is one thing that all humans have in common. The "advanced" societies have broken it down into days, hours and seconds; the "primitives" into moons and seasons. But for all of us time is eternal. We do not start and end, we start and go on. Whether we measure time in moons or light-years, we are accountable for our use of our portion of it. Our actions in our splotch of time create a ripple effect throughout eternity.

For a person who does not have the assurance of an eternity with God, time is an enemy, slowly creeping and then suddenly pouncing. For those who know Christ as Lord it is not a commodity to be wasted. It is an opportunity to be used to bring glory to God.

Read Psalm 90.

Underline the verses that give us hope and encouragement in light of our limited time on earth.

What does verse 12 mean? (If you can't figure it out make sure that you ask someone, look it up in a Bible commentary or read it in another version of the Bible.)

Describe a "wise" way to live when you realize that our days are "numbered."

Day 2 Time to Grow Up

I pulled open a drawer the other day and there they were—little army men, guns drawn, the good guys and the bad guys. What memories they bring. I used to sit for hours and play with them. I'd take half the day to set them up and the other half to systematically knock them down. And pity the poor brother or sister who "helped" bring the troops to a premature death.

Scratching around the drawer a little more I found other mementos of times gone by—an old tube of model glue, some paints and a few spare model parts. I could never figure out where they went. Some old records—badges, magnets and a magnifying glass—odds and ends of childhood. Man! I loved that stuff. I lived just to play with it. Now it is sitting in a box, waiting for another kid down the block, a grandchild or the Goodwill. Even though I loved that stuff I don't really want to play with it. I've grown up.

We laugh at the goofy pictures of ourselves as kids. In ten years we'll laugh again at pictures of ourselves now. Time and wisdom are making us mature.

As a child I cared about the things that matter only to children; this was right, for children should not have to shoulder the burdens of adults. Now that I'm an adult it is harder and harder for me to care about the things that a child would care about. It is not just growing old, it is growing up. Unfortunately, this is something that does not come as naturally with the years as one would expect.

Maturity is not just losing the desire for the toys of childhood. It involves other things such as character, faith, love and a godly perspective on life. It is all too possible to grow old but not grow up.

It happens when one refuses or fails to come to grips with the crucial issues of life. When one confuses muscle and strength with manhood, shape and complexion with womanhood, power and possessions with maturity. Shaving, drinking, working, marrying and bearing children are marks of growing older, not necessarily signs of growing up. They are not to be confused with maturity. In fact, there are many adults who handle life in exactly the same way as they handled it in their childhood. The difference is that the stakes are bigger and the people are real, not imaginary.

The time for dolls and action figures is most likely over for you. It is time to grow up—or at least time to start growing up. We never quite get all the way grown up in this life—that is left for eternity. (After all, you have to have something to do there.)

Read 1 Corinthians 13. What does this passage tell you about growing up? What are some qualities that time should build into you if you seek wisdom?

Day 3 Time and Eternity

There are certain sayings which cultures develop so as to put into a sentence a whole philosophy, a way of looking at and dealing with some aspect of life. We call them proverbs, adages, epigrams, or even clichés. They are often repeated and seldom really mentally weighed. Some of them are essentially true, but their meaning can be twisted and bent. If a saying finds its way into some advertising slogan it can be used to state an idea that is very much untrue.

Many adages deal with the subject of time. Most are designed to spur us to action and shake our complacency.

One example is a modern cliché that says, "You only go around once in life, so grab all the gusto you can." At first this sounds like good advice. It is certainly true that we will not be given a repeat performance at living our life. It is true that we should use to the best advantage the opportunities that come our way. But this saying goes wrong when it implies that we must reach out and seize all the pleasure we can carry because we will never have the chance again. This reflects a point of view that looks at this world only. It is shortsighted in terms of eternity. For in God's plan we will have all eternity to enjoy the pleasures He will provide.

For every pregnancy terminated because that new life would interfere with the self-fulfilling life-style of the mother, there is a small baby who pays for that self-fulfillment.

For every barrel of hatred leveled at the social or physical weaknesses of another individual there are unheard sobs at night.

For every misuse of resources, of our bodies or the bodies of others, of our tongue, our talent or even of our relationships, there is a price to pay now or in the future. Time on this earth is only a fraction of our existence. What we do here has eternal consequences.

Will God hold us accountable for a world famine eighty years from now, because we neglected to share our skill, concern and technology as a nation or as individuals with others who could have put them to use? Will our children and grandchildren be raised in the ruins of a valueless society because we did not have the time to speak to others about the only One who gives true and everlasting values? Will we produce generation after generation of spiritual dwarfs, lulled into the contentment of gathering up pleasures for themselves, seeking the instant thrill rather than paying the dues for things that may not produce immediate rewards?

The alternative is hard but necessary. We must live as though life counts for eternity—because it does.

Read Proverbs 24:30-34.

What are some of the "fields" you might have neglected in order to do what you wanted to do?

This passage speaks of being lazy and negligent. Identify areas where you tend to seek your own pleasure without thinking of the consequences.

Day 4 We're Watching You

In our culture we are surrounded by a vast (and increasing) display of technical wizardry that has changed the way people live, think, learn and respond. The most dynamic of the electronic intruders has been television.

By the age of 65, the average American will have spent at least nine years of his or her life watching television. This is a phenomenal amount of time! Think of the skill an artist or musician could develop by devoting nine years to study. Think of the relationships that could be developed with nine years of being together.

Television is a *passive* form of entertainment (like watching a sports event or a concert). While passive entertainment may be a very good way to relax and enjoy the skills of another, for some it replaces personal creative ventures. Some critics of television even believe that it has a stranglehold on our culture, threatening to smother the creativity and imagination in all but a few. Some fear that we are doomed to live in a spectator world—watching things happen and never making them happen ourselves.

Perhaps another danger of passive entertainment is the very high level of professionalism expected of its performers. The beginning musician, writer, dancer or journalist may feel overwhelmed with inferiority by comparison. Budding skills may be abandoned because the performer is surrounded by those who do so much better.

For others the danger lies in the use of television and video as a drug, blotting out boredom, filling in the blank time in the day rather than relying on creativity and imagination. Problems are not solved, but merely forgotten for a time.

Still another objection is aimed at the lack of moral standards demonstrated on many programs. Creators of TV shows usually say that the programs are "amoral," not "immoral" in philosophy. The difference between the two is difficult to define. Adultery, cheating, violence and intemperance are often shown as the norm. The danger here is that simplistic ideas and dramatic endings make good entertainment—but lousy reality. The message communicated is that totally unacceptable behavior is in fact acceptable.

Obviously the glowing tube is not the only means of escape that is used. Records, radio, tapes, video games and other high tech playthings can also produce a person who would rather observe than act.

While watching, listening and playing are not wrong, we must take active steps to control what we take in—not only in terms of quality but also in quantity.

In a world where people are thought of as consumers, audiences, the buying public or numbers in a computer, the members of the Christian community must be pushing towards a different goal. If the whole world drifts towards an aimless void of spectatorism we must not float with them. The people of the Cross should be different. We should be active, imaginative, interesting and ultimately out of step with the masses. This path eventually is not only much more uplifting, it is also much more entertaining.

Read James 1:22-26. How do some people become "religious spectators"? Why do you think it might be easier to slip into this sin today than in James's day? Make a list of things that you could actively *do* in the time spent in over-indulgence of spectatorism.

Day 5 "Time-Packing"

Imagine that you have the job of packing a truck for a long journey. In the warehouse where you are working, you have more than enough materials to fill this vehicle five times over. Suppose also that you are left with the job of loading this truck without much supervision or help.

Many people would load the truck by impulse rather than by planning. They would tend to stack things up in a random and arbitrary manner and then proceed to fill the truck with those things.

Now suppose that you were to have the help of a professional packer in loading your truck—a person who had thought out the best way to get the most goods into the space available. Such a person could probably pack the truck with twice as much material as the rest of us. (For a graphic illustration try packing your suitcase with care and thought, and then packing it again by randomly throwing your stuff in. There will be quite a difference in the results.)

In many ways the truck can be an allegory of our lives when it comes to time. We have the potential to pack many great events and experiences into a lifetime if we take some care to learn how to properly "pack" our time. Instead many of us live life at random, never learning how to load each day to the maximum.

The care and caution with which we plan each day determines how much we can accomplish. It is interesting to observe people who have the idea of proper "time-packing." They live the lives of three individuals by what they do and accomplish. Good use of our time makes our lives richer.

There are some very important tips that can help us with godly time management. First we must have our priorities right. God and the things that are important to Him must be most important to us. We must not just make time for God, we must make Him God of our time. Since other people are important to God, we must not get too busy to talk, share and even play with those God has placed around us.

We need goals that are realistic to reach each day, month, and year, along with a good dose of self-control so that we don't do what we feel like doing but what we need to be doing.

Some tools, such as calendars, lists of things to do and

such reminders, can help. (Don't trust your memory to carry you through busy times.)

As we stack the parcels that are the important gifts and pleasures in life, we do not have to throw out recreation, relaxation and goofing off just to be assured of a full life. We simply need to take some thought and intentionally place those things, rather than letting them come to rest "any old way" they land. With a little thinking and organization our lives become fuller and more productive not only for us but also for the King we serve.

Read Matthew 25:14-30.

Imagine that the talents given were portions of time—days, weeks, or months. If you were one of the servants, how would you get the most from your time?

Day 6 There's a Time for Everything

Have you ever noticed that no matter how badly you want summer to come, it always takes its own sweet time getting here? The seasons are not speeded by our anxiety. God has locked them into cycles that will not vary to accommodate our schedules or wants. In fact, we expect things to be this way. We would be more than a little shook up if the seasons began to determine their own schedule. Imagine a two-week summer followed by a nine-month winter! We know that there is a fixed amount of time for each season, and ultimately we are glad for it.

There is a time and a season for things other than the weather. There is a time when you live with your family and must be obedient to your parents. Some wish to squeeze the season of this time much shorter than God has intended.

There is a time for learning, acquiring knowledge and experience—for paying our dues by scrubbing the toilet at the local fast food restaurant before we can be involved in more "refined" types of employment.

There is a time for growing and learning about the feelings and needs of other people before we take the giant step of spending the rest of our lives with one special person. Many want to reduce the length of that season, thereby leading to the radical divorce rate experienced today even among Christians.

There is a time for waiting patiently for God, and for hearing and doing before taking on the responsibilities of leadership.

There are times and seasons for these things to take place. They must not be rushed or the harvest will suffer.

The key to everything said here is this: *Take your time.* If the person you love loves you, he or she will wait for you. A job worth having is worth spending the time to prepare for. Take your time being a child. (That may sound very silly, but if you are able to spend time being a kid while you are a kid, you will be less likely to try to recapture that lost childhood when you are an adult.)

Take time to know who it is you serve, why you serve Him and how this affects your present and your future—before you try to determine its direction.

Take time to know people as real people. They have a lot to teach, a lot to give, and much to receive from you.

Take the time to do the job of living right.

Read Ecclesiastes 3:1-9.

Circle phrases that describe experiences that you have had a season of so far.

R.B.

Wisdom with Words

Day 1 The Power of Words

Once there was a young man who came into a great inheritance through the death of a rich uncle. With the great sums of cash bequeathed to him, he bought all the necessary equipment with which to establish a farm and a life of his own. He loaded these things onto a ship and set out to find a place where he could carry out his plans unimpeded by his father, who managed nevertheless to deliver one last piece of advice as the heavily-laden vessel was leaving port. "Son," he said, "keep your hand on the rudder!"

"Don't worry," the young man replied. "I know where I'm

going!" So the ship began slowly to make its way through the harbor, past the great sailing vessels of many lands which had come to unload their varied cargoes. But just as the ship was nearly free of the harbor, the young man let go of the rudder to pour himself another glass of champagne, and smashed into the yacht of the visiting king of Kazmovia. Neither vessel sank, but the young man's ship had to be sold to pay for the damage to the king's yacht, with nothing left him but one horse and a few farm implements.

The young man's father graciously overlooked his son's foolishness and gave him several acres of prime land, including a small farmhouse and a barn. Again, the father had just one word of advice for his son as preparation was being made to begin plowing the acreage. "Make sure that the bit is firmly in place," he said. "That horse of yours has a wild look in his eye."

"I know! I know!" the son replied impatiently, as the horse careened into a ditch, breaking a leg and throwing the young man and his plow into a deep pond of thick mud. The poor horse had to be destroyed, and with no way of retrieving the plow, it too was lost.

Now, with nothing left but a house, a barn and a plot of land which he had no way to use, the young man resorted to candle-making as a way of turning his last resources into a profit. For the third time, the father was on hand with a word of advice as the young man was busy converting the barn into a candle-making shop. "Watch the sparks from your fire, son; this hay is awfully dry!"

Again, the young man was quick with an impatient reply: "Why don't you mind your own business?" he snapped. "Don't you think I know anything?"

That night, the young man was busy making his first batch of candles. Meanwhile the fire roared and the wax bubbled furiously. A tiny spark flew into a pile of hay and soon the entire barn was engulfed in flames, followed quickly by the farmhouse. The young man lost everything but his life. His entire fortune had been wiped out by three small mistakes.

Could such things as this really happen? Would anyone be so foolish as to sail a ship with no rudder, or drive a horse with no bit? Would anyone let live sparks fly into a haystack? Certainly such things would be unthinkable. But there is something very much like the things in this story that is often just as carelessly misused, something just as powerful in its effect as a rudder, or a bit, or a spark. It's something that everybody has—a tongue.

In the third chapter of James, the tongue is compared to the rudder of a ship, the bit of a horse, and a fiery spark. Whoever can control this troublesome member is capable of controlling his entire person. He is a "perfect" man. But how does a person acquire the skill needed for such an impossible task? Proverbs 16:20 gives the answer to that question. "Whoever gives heed to instruction prospers, and blessed is he who trusts in the Lord." The young man in our story could have avoided disaster if he had listened to the advice of his father. We too have the benefit of the perfect advice of our Father in heaven, but it is useless *unless we are willing to listen to it.*

Words can improve the morale or wound it (see Prov. 12:18). They can flatter to the point of injury (see 29:5), or spread blessing to many (see 10:21). Words even have the power to affect bodily health (see 16:24; 15:30). Proverbs 18:21 sums up the whole matter and puts James's message in a nutshell: "The tongue has the power of life and death . . . . "

Take a moment to ask yourself whether you are *truly willing* to listen to what God has to say to you about your own use of words. Are you ready to do what He says, or are you ready to give a quick reply like the foolish young man?

Read James 3:1-12 and see what God says about the tongue and its awesome power.

What examples of wrong use of words are given by James?

List ways words can be used for good.

What reason does James give for not cursing people (see v. 9)?

Day 2 The Weakness of Words

It's no surprise that a book of wise sayings would have a lot to do with the power of words. But Proverbs also contains some important reminders about the weakness of words. As powerful as they are, there are some things that words most definitely cannot do. For instance, words cannot serve as a substitute for deeds.

"Hello, may I speak with Mr. Ailsworth please? Hello Mr. Ailsworth, this is Thelma Crisp from Atlantic Stereo. Do you remember that check you wrote us for $789? It just came back from the bank. That's right, it bounced. Would you come in some time today and pay this in cash?"

Mr. Ailsworth's problem is not unusual. People quite frequently write checks for more money than they have in the bank. Most do it by accident, some do it on purpose. Those who make a habit of doing it deliberately often end up in jail. Apart from the world of finance, people "write bad checks" by making commitments they cannot keep, or by spouting all sorts of idealistic talk that isn't followed by any corresponding behavior.

For example, it's very fashionable in some circles these days to talk about world hunger. But handing over the cash to feed those hungry people is not nearly so easy as talking about it. And apparently it was no easier two thousand years ago, for this particular brand of words without deeds is addressed specifically in the second chapter of James.

Very few people *deliberately* write checks for more than they have in the bank, because they know that some person or machine is keeping an exact account of every penny. But when we "write bad checks" to God by talking and then not doing, we shouldn't be surprised to find that He also has a way of counting everything. Proverbs 24:12 talks about our accountability: "Will he not repay each person according to what he has done?"

Proverbs 14:23 puts it firmly and succinctly: "All hard work brings a profit, but mere talk leads only to poverty." Can you think of a specific instance in the last week where you said something that was just as worthless as a bad check? Are you prepared with some "cash" to make good on it?

For more on the subject of words without deeds read James 2:14-26. James is not saying that you cannot be saved by faith. He is saying that true faith is accompanied by what?

James gives a man and a woman as examples of people who supported their words with deeds. Who are they? What were their deeds? Would their deeds make them a hero/heroine in your community? Why or why not?

Day 3 The Best Words Are Apt

"A man finds joy in giving an apt reply—and how good is a timely word!" (Prov. 15:23)

It is a 7:05 A.M. You are in surgery for a brain transplant. Several people in green gowns are huddled around you, all holding on to something or other. At 7:06 the chief surgeon says, "Prepare for disconnection of the medicular axiomis."

"Ready," comes a terse reply from the assisting surgeon.

Several people change positions to prepare for the climax of a procedure which has yet to be completed successfully with a human being. Now everyone in the room stands frozen as the chief surgeon watches the seconds tick by. Then comes the following exchange:

"Ready . . . now!"
"Medicular axiomis disconnected."
"Initiate perinubrial autolocation."
"Initiated . . . and complete."

The procedure is successful. The chief surgeon steps back, removes his gloves and issues a few last instructions.

The result of all this is that you are still alive. If you had been awake through it all you would now have a special appreciation for the well-timed word that we call *apt*. If the words spoken by the chief surgeon were not spoken at precisely the right moment, they might have lost their power to preserve your life. How unfortunate that so many of *our* best words, wise and true though they may be, are simply spoken at the wrong time! They are *inapt*.

You are seated at a table in the most expensive restaurant in town, celebrating your speedy recovery. Tantalizing and exotic odors are making their way from the kitchen to your table, eliciting exquisite pangs of hunger from you and your guests. Finally, after a seemingly endless wait, your food arrives and is set before you. "Ahhh!" You sigh with pleasure as you eagerly work your fork and knife. You pop the first bite into your mouth and your expression turns from ecstasy to disgust. The cook has poured chocolate sauce over your prime rib.

It's an easy mistake to make. The chocolate sauce is in a double boiler, right next to the beef gravy. And you're not the only one with problems; the woman at the next table is in for her own surprise, gravy on ice cream.

There was nothing wrong with the chocolate sauce. On the contrary, it was made with the finest ingredients. But that velvety confection was unwelcome because it didn't fit the occasion. How unfortunate that in so many critical situations we fail to choose the best *words* to fit the occasion. Again, our words are *inapt*.

Remember the face you made when you ate a bite of that

roast beef with chocolate sauce on it? (Use your imagination.) If you try hard enough, you might be able to remember a time when your mother or father made the same face in response to an ill-timed remark from you! Try to think of at least one example of these two kinds of inapt words: (1) the right word that came at the wrong time, (2) the word that was altogether wrong for the circumstances.

If you find it hard to come up with your own examples, try these on for size:

It's perfectly fine to let your sister know about the straight A's on *your* report card. But not when she's still in tears over her own failing grade in geometry.

How admirable of you to tell your mother that her boss, old Mr. Grundy, doesn't smell at all like month-old gym socks! But shouldn't you wait till the old gaffer has gotten at least halfway to his car?

No doubt almost everyone in the family is interested in every detail of how the vet punctured and drained the cat's abscess. It might be better received though, if you wait till dinner is over to give your report.

Day 4 The Best Words Are Honest

"Good morning, class! Please turn to chapter eight in your textbooks and find diagram three. Today we will be studying the anatomy of a lie. Now, starting here with the anterior surface of the transverse motive, you will notice that there is a direct connection with the lateral face of the descending profit factor, which is attached to the modus operandi by way of . . . "

Yes, it would be nice if the entire phenomenon called dishonesty could be so plainly visualized like a diagram in a biology textbook. Unfortunately, we don't have it so easy. We must dissect this slimy specimen with words.

People lie for many different reasons. Sometimes a lie is materially profitable; sometimes the profit is less tangible. We'll be talking about one particular type of non-material profit that often leads people into dishonesty: social profit.

How many times have you lied about your achievements in order to make a good impression with your family or friends? Was that long touchdown pass really seventy-five yards? Was your test score really the highest in the whole class? Do you really make $100 a week at your part-time job? Maybe you haven't exaggerated about any of these things. But at some time you've probably exaggerated about something.

Since the beginning of time, people have had the urge to exaggerate their deeds in order to improve their social standing or to enhance their self-worth. It's a vice that almost everyone finds irresistible at some time or other.

Take Ananias and Sapphira, for example (see Acts 5). They were members of the Bethel Avenue Christian Fellowship in Jerusalem. Many of the members there had sold property and given the proceeds to the church. The money was normally presented to Peter, the senior pastor. Ananias and his wife wanted everyone in the church to admire their great faith and generosity. So they sold some property too; only their faith wasn't really all that great, and they didn't want to part with all the proceeds. So they secretly kept part of the money for themselves, and brought the remainder to the pastor. Peter saw through their deception and, in so many words, told them to drop dead (which they most obligingly did).

What would the couple have gained if their trick had gone unnoticed? They would have gained the unmerited admiration of Peter and the congregation of Bethel Avenue, when they should have been concerned only with God's approval in the first place. (Jesus said that the approval of people is our *only* reward if that's all we're aiming for.) But Ananias and Sapphira didn't fool God, and couldn't have, even if they had fooled everyone else.

This type of dishonesty stems mainly from our desire to make people believe all sorts of wonderful things about us when the truth is that we are actually rather average. Maybe Ananias and Sapphira never had the kinds of friends who accepted them just the way they were. In any case, Peter was quite irritated with these two parishioners. Had their lie been unplanned, he might have gone a little easier on them, because Peter himself had been guilty of some impulsive dishonesty of his own.

It happened like this: At the last supper, Jesus told His disciples that He was about to be crucified, and warned His followers that they would scatter. But Peter was undaunted; he was confident that this warning applied to everyone except himself. "I am ready to go with you to prison and to death." He said. "Even if I have to die with you, I will never disown you" (Luke 22:33; Mark 14:31). But when the pressure was on, Peter faltered. A servant girl thought she recognized him. "I don't know what you're talking about," he insisted with oaths and curses. "I don't know the man!" (see Matt. 26:70,74). He had underestimated his own will to survive. His affiliation with Christ was finally given away; not by the words he spoke, but by the dialect of his speech.

Sounds familiar? How about the time you kept silent when some of your friends were making fun of that oddball, Jeff, who "goes to church every Sunday with his Mommy and Daddy"? You wanted to be accepted by certain people and thought it would be disadvantageous to make a "controversial" reply. Perhaps you soon forgot about it. But as soon as Peter realized what he had done, he broke down and wept.

Americans rarely lose their lives confessing allegiance to Christ. So what *do* they lose? Their losses are usually social. They lose the approval of some individual or group. They suffer embarrassment. Social survival is so important to some of us that we guard it as if our very lives were at stake. But who would want to be in the company of people who would ostracize someone for being a Christian? Who would want to be identified with any "in" group that is so at odds with the very center of our lives?

Some readers will say, "Not me! I don't care for the approval of any 'in' group! I'm just going to be myself and tell the truth, including the fact of my faith in Christ!" But all of us are a little bit like Peter. We forget the strength of our will to survive socially, and under pressure often find ourselves leaving the path of commitment. That doesn't mean we should be insensitive or reckless in our dealings with non-believers. It doesn't mean that diplomacy goes out the window. It *does* mean that if the only motive behind our words is to avoid social embarrassment, then we are no better than cowards, and subject to the warning of Jesus in Luke 9:26: "If anyone is ashamed of me and my words, the Son of Man will be ashamed of him."

Whether we profit socially or materially, the fact remains that any kind of dishonest profit is temporary and full of poison. Some lies are planned, others come at a moment of weakness. But there is one feature in the anatomy of a lie that occurs consistently: The motive is always firmly attached to some kind of gain.

Proverbs 21:6, then, applies to all kinds of lies: "A fortune made by a lying tongue is a fleeting vapor and a deadly snare." See if you can apply this verse to yourself with the help of these questions:

1. When are you most likely to exaggerate about yourself?
2. What do you think you stand to gain by it?
3. How does your interest in social gain affect your ability to talk openly about your faith?
4. What changes would you like to make in this area of your life?

Day 5 The Best Words Are Calm

"A gentle answer turns away wrath, but a harsh word stirs up anger" (Prov. 15:1). This must be one of the most practical statements in the whole book of Proverbs. And few would deny the truth of it. Self-control, though, is needed to implement it, and that's where most of us get caught. We often respond with hasty words the way people on a diet respond to the smell of an apple pie as it comes out of the oven. All the correct intentions are there, but some parts of our brains care little for good intentions. So we act on impulse. And before we know it, we have done just the opposite of what we intended. "Clink!" goes the fork onto the empty plate.

Judges 7 and 8 contain a splendid account of how the use of gentle words can defuse an otherwise volatile situation. In Judges 7, Gideon, with an army of only three hundred men, had surprised the Midianite army and driven it into the hands of Gideon's fellow countrymen in Ephraim. The men of Ephraim finished off the Midianite army, captured its two leaders, and then joined Gideon. But the Ephraimites were insulted because they hadn't been called in to fight at the beginning. By the time they met with Gideon they were fuming.

"Why have you treated us like this?" they asked. "Why didn't you call us when you went to fight Midian?"

At this point, Gideon could have delivered any number of terse replies. He had been appointed by God and given explicit instructions to trim his army of thirty-two thousand men and go to battle with only three hundred. He could have said, "Who put you in charge of me so that my every move could be questioned and challenged? Where were you when the angel of the Lord appointed me to lead the armies of Israel into battle against the Midianites and their allies? Do you dare to question the wisdom of the Lord and His instruction?"

Gideon might have been justified in making such a response. He didn't have to answer to the men of Ephraim! But this was his reply: "What have I accomplished compared to you? . . . God gave Oreb and Zeeb, the Midianite leaders, into your hands. What was I able to do compared to you?" (Judg. 8:2,3). At this, the men of Ephraim forgot their anger; "their resentment subsided." You can picture them, a whole army, putting their swords back in their sheaths one by one. And that's what Proverbs 15:1 is all about, choosing words which will cause our enemies to put away their swords.

One harsh word from Gideon, justified though it might have been, could have resulted in violence and death. One harsh word to a friend or family member can be just as serious, sometimes inflicting as much injury and pain as the sword.

Some people seem to have more self-control than others. Some seem to have excellent intentions and yet never follow through with them under pressure. But practice makes perfect, and the use of gentle words is an art that comes easier the more it is practiced.

The choice of one word has often been pivotal to the outcome of some of the most important events in history. Take a few minutes and see if you can think of any events in your own life over the past year that could have been changed with one word. If your memory fails you, think of a hypothetical situation in which you are engaged in a heated discussion with a member of your family. Use your imagination and let the conversation run its usual course. Then, try substituting gentle words for some that might be on the harsh side. See how these alternate words might change the course of such a conversation. Make a note of the kinds of words you substitute and try them out the next time you find yourself in such a situation. Remember, the use of gentle words requires practice!

This is one way of getting it.

Day 6 Words Reveal Character

"Even a fool is thought wise if he keeps silent, and discern-ing if he holds his tongue . . . [his] mouth is his undoing, and his lips are a snare to his soul" (Prov. 17:28; 18:7).

Yes, even *you* can be considered wise and discerning! All you have to do is keep your mouth shut! But alas, that's like trying to catch a bird by sprinkling salt on its tail. If you can get that close, the bird is as good as caught. And if you are wise enough to keep silent, you've earned your reputation.

Unfortunately, even fools must communicate to others through language. You could take an oath of silence and live in a monastery. But most people brave it out and take their chances in the real world of words and fools.

You are transparent. It's an unavoidable fact. You will be exposed by the things you say. If you are wise, people will know it. If you are foolish, they'll know that just as well. Few of us, though, are either wise or foolish all the time. Most of us maintain an average that we hope is above the level of total folly. This average could be called our character. It is the sum of all the facets of our personality. And every one of these facets is exposed by our words.

If you are a loving person, the fact will be known. If you are self-centered, people will see it just as clearly as if you adver-tise it on the biggest billboard in town. If you have joy and peace, it will be written in large letters over everything you say. If you are full of hate, it will escape from your mouth the way acid oozes out of an old battery. If you are gentle and kind, it will come out, even in the way you report the time of day or give a baseball score.

You can't hide your true self any more than a herd of elephants can hide behind a bamboo pole. Sooner or later you will be caught with your mouth open, being yourself.

So there's only one thing to do if you don't want to look like a fool, and that is to stop being one. Easier said than done? Sure; but there's hope, and it starts at the beginning of Proverbs. Remember? "The fear of the Lord is the beginning of knowledge, but fools despise wisdom and discipline" (Prov. 1:7).

That's the answer to your own foolishness. If you fear God, if you truly respect Him, and genuinely believe that everything He says is true, then you are wiser than you can imagine. The very epitome of foolishness is to reject the Word of God, His own wisdom, and the provision to be made righteous in His eyes. But when you accept God and the partnership He offers, you have the assurance Paul talks about in Philippians 1:6: "He who began a good work in you will carry it on to completion until the day of Christ Jesus."

God wants to work with you to make you into the sort of person whose words are not dangerous or insensitive or foolish, but rather edifying and constructive and appropriate. But you must volunteer to participate in this remodeling project. To find out how, read James 1:5.

Here's an exercise to get rid of unwanted foolishness. Do you have areas in your life where you tend to resist instruction? See how many verses in the book of Proverbs you can find that address these areas specifically. You might want to underline some of them so they'll catch your eye again. Or you might choose the best two or three and commit them to memory. This can be an effective sort of vaccination against foolish habits and thought patterns.

D.E.

Wisdom with Wealth

Day 1 The Wise Use of Money

"The Millionaire" was a popular TV show some years ago. In each episode the show would start with a man carrying a briefcase and walking up to a door. He would knock on the door or ring the doorbell. When the person inside would answer, this man would say, "Hello, you don't know me, but I represent a millionaire who prefers to remain anonymous. I have a check made out in your name in the amount of one million dollars." He would then hand over the check and walk away. The rest of the program focused on what the person did with the money. Some would save it, some would give it away, some would spend it all.

Have you ever thought about what you would do with a million dollars? The book of Proverbs has a lot to say about money and how to use it wisely. Most of the book was written by King Solomon, one of the richest and wisest people who ever lived. Even though we may never be millionaires, we would do well to take Solomon's advice on the wise use of money.

One theme that is strong in Proverbs is summed up this way: "Better a little with righteousness than much gain with injustice" (Prov. 16:8). It's better to be satisfied with the little that you can earn honorably than to get involved in shady deals. It's better to earn an honest C than to cheat for an A. While those who are dishonest may seem to make short-term gains, in the long run—in God's perspective—the honest will be much better off.

Another bit of wisdom that is stressed in Proverbs is this: "He who gives to the poor will lack nothing, but he who closes his eyes to them receives many curses" (Prov. 28:27). God expects us to use our resources compassionately—to care for those less fortunate than ourselves. This might take the form of giving part of our allowance or earnings to a church ministry to the poor. It might mean spending time with a kid at school whose family doesn't have much money—a kid who is shunned by others because he or she doesn't have the latest designer jeans or status-symbol shirt. It might mean treating a friend to lunch instead of spending all our money on ourselves. This sort of generosity will be rewarded! (See Prov. 11:24,25.)

Another rather interesting wise use of money is to use it to make opportunities. "A gift opens the way for the giver . . . " (Prov. 18:16). This is not a bribe, but a gift that shows that the giver is generous and gracious and worthy of friendship. Sometimes a generous act such as a gift can spark a relationship that eventually will allow you to share your faith with the other person.

The wise use of money also involves the right attitude about money. The Bible makes it very plain that the key to happiness is not wealth, but contentment with what you have. Take a look at 1 Timothy 6:6-19. Read what it has to say about riches and the attitude of contentment. What are some things we must avoid? What are some things we are to do? And in what are we supposed to put our hope?

Finally, look at the prayer in Proverbs 30:8,9. What does it say?

Day 2 You Can't Take It with You

Lee was a guy with a lot of musical talent. All through high school and college he had played in bands, performing at parties, nightclubs, concerts, and so on. But Lee knew that making it big was hard to do in the music industry, so he became a business major in college. In his senior year he opened a small record store near the college, and soon the business took off. Within two years he opened another store in the same town. Things continued to grow. Two record stores soon became four, and then eight stores in three different cities. As his business empire continued to grow, Lee got wealthier and wealthier. To most of his friends Lee was the picture of success.

Lee's best friend from his old band and his former girl friend had both become Christians in college. All along they had tried to tell Lee about Jesus, but he was always too busy. "I don't have time for God right now," Lee would tell his friends. And then he would run off to band practice, class or the opening of a new record store.

Lee's friends threw him a surprise party for his twenty-ninth birthday. Following the fun, food and presents, and after everyone had gone, Lee sat and thought about where he was.

"I'll have fun for a few years and really live it up, then I'll settle down, get married and get into God," he thought.

But God looked at Lee and said, "You fool. This very night your life will be demanded from you. Then who will get what you have prepared for yourself?"

Jesus told a story a lot like this. It's recorded in Luke 12:16-21. At the end He says, "This is how it will be with anyone who stores up things for himself but is not rich toward God."

There are many people who are caught in the trap of trusting in their riches. They feel that money can save them from anything. Proverbs 18:11 talks about how foolish this is. "The wealth of the rich is their fortified city; they imagine it an unscaleable wall." They don't realize that all of their money and possessions are of no use to them once they stand before God.

Proverbs 11:4 reads, "Wealth is worthless in the day of wrath, but righteousness delivers from death."

The Bible makes it clear that we are not to put our trust in riches, but in God. Proverbs 11:28 says, "Whoever trusts in his riches will fall, but the righteous will thrive like a green leaf." We are to be concerned with righteousness and pleasing God rather than building riches and pleasing ourselves.

Look at Jesus' comments recorded in Matthew 6:19-21. What treasures are you laying up on earth? What treasures are you laying up in heaven? Where would you have to say your heart really is?

Day 3 Generosity

One of the most popular and colorful stories of Charles Dickens is "A Christmas Carol." The story is about the transformation of Ebenezer Scrooge, a greedy old man who cares nothing for his neighbors or his employees. He has no friends. Only after he has an encounter with three ghosts who show him his past, his present and his future does he change. And what a change! Scrooge ends up becoming the most generous and the most beloved man in the whole town.

In much the same way one of the marks of the Christian is generosity. A Christian learns to delight in giving to others. The Bible says, "If anyone has material possessions and sees his brother in need but has no pity on him, how can the love of God be in him?" (1 John 3:17). When Jesus takes over a person's life, that person wants to share with others.

The book of Proverbs has a lot to say about generosity and giving. It makes a number of promises—not only to those who help the poor but also to those who refuse to help. For example, "He who gives to the poor will lack nothing, but he who closes his eyes to them receives many curses" (Prov. 28:27). Another example is: "If a man shuts his ears to the cry of the poor, he too will cry out and not be answered" (Prov. 21:13). God has strong feelings about those who refuse to help people less fortunate than themselves.

On the other side, blessings are promised to those who give help to the needy. Proverbs 11:25,26 reads, "A generous man will prosper; he who refreshes others will himself be refreshed. People curse the man who hoards grain, but blessings crown him who is willing to sell."

The one who is willing to be generous toward others is favored by those whom he helps, and also by God. Proverbs 14:21 says, "He who despises his neighbor sins, but blessed is he who is kind to the needy." Jesus said, "I was hungry and you gave me something to eat, I was thirsty and you gave me something to drink, I was a stranger and you invited me in, I needed clothes and you clothed me, I was sick and you looked after me, I was in prison and you came to visit me" (Matt. 25:35,36). The people had done these things, not directly for Jesus Himself, but for those whom He loves deeply: the poor, the homeless, the unwanted, the unloved. To be generous to them is to be kind to the Lord and show our love for Him. Proverbs 19:17 reads, "He who is kind to the poor lends to the Lord, and he will reward him for what he has done."

Who do you know who is less fortunate than yourself? What is one way you can be generous toward that person? Money and food are only two ways. What about the need for love and attention? Or the need to be listened to? Think of some ways that you can reach out to people Jesus loves.

Day 4 Wisdom to Know What Is Better

A common saying states, "Every man has his price." This implies that if the "carrot" is large enough a person will do just about anything. While most would protest this thought, insisting that they are the exception, it is an interesting idea to think about. Is there a price to our morality?

If someone offered us several million dollars in cash to tell a lie—and displayed the money before our very eyes—can we be sure that we would not do it?

Many would reply, "It depends on the lie." In that case, those people do have a price tag on their morality, since they would consider doing something wrong in order to benefit from the deed.

There was a memorable scene in a film made a number of years ago. *The Magic Christian* showed a wealthy person who was trying to prove that people would do anything for money. He threw piles of cash into a cesspool and laughed as people plunged into the filth to retrieve the money. A Christian who gladly dives into a cesspool of sin in order to increase his or her wealth is not so far removed from that scene!

It is unfortunate but true that some Christian business

people have become so entranced by the accumulation of things that they have forgotten the spiritual principles that are supposed to govern their lives and their use of money. They employ all manner of fraud and deception in order to increase their profit, and in the process they make their "witness" a joke to those with whom they have dealings.

Jesus said that we should seek God's kingdom first, and then we would receive the necessities of life (see Matt. 6:28-33). In some cases God blesses far beyond mere necessities. But other people reach out for a level of wealth that God does not intend them to have. They fall into a trap as they abandon their spiritual responsibilities in order to benefit financially.

Before you insist that you are immune to this disease, think carefully about how big a "carrot" it would take for you to do something unpleasant, humiliating, embarrassing or even wrong. Some who try this might realize that they would sell out for far less than they originally thought.

Read the passages from Proverbs indicated here and list the things they say are more important than money. What can you add to this list from other Scripture not given here? Proverbs 15:16; 16:8; 17:16; 20:15; 22:1,2; 23:4,5; 28:6.

Day 5 The Wisdom of Hard Work

A shabby man wandered into the church office and told a tale of unemployment and bad luck, of hunger pangs and sleeping on park benches. The pastor heard him out, then gave him a few dollars for a meal.

Most churches maintain some sort of benevolent fund from which staff members may draw cash to help strangers or other people who have hit hard times. Some, rather than giving cash, maintain accounts with a local restaurant and lodging place in order to help those in need.

Needless to say, there are people who know how to "work" this system of charity and who live entirely by drifting from one church to another begging a handout. They are pros.

Some churches have established a policy with regard to charity. They will gladly give assistance to a needy stranger in exchange for work. The task usually involves something like working on the grounds of the church, keeping the weeds from taking over the parking lot. It is amazing how many desperate needs evaporate when the mention of work comes up. In fact, it is not unusual for the stranger to "cuss out" the staff person and give him or her a lecture about Christian love.

Of course, churches that offer to help in exchange for work are acting on firm biblical principles: "If a man will not work, he shall not eat" (2 Thess. 3:10). Earning our way is a godly principle that even applies to people who still live with parents.

God not only states that work is necessary, He gives some hearty advice about the amount of effort that we put into it. Hard work pays off! Naturally, our priorities must be right. We must not be slaves to the dollar nor negligent of higher priorities such as family, fellowship, service and worship. We should avoid becoming workaholics. But when at work we must be diligent. The payoff comes in a number of ways. It can be economic—raises and advances. Or it can be self-respect, knowing that we have done a good job. The payoff might be physical well-being (especially when the work requires physical labor). It might be a good testimony among those we work with. It might be productivity that gives glory to God. It might be the satisfaction of developing honesty, responsibility and trustworthiness—all of which are part of the Christian experience that must be translated from Bible study to the real world.

Hard work will not necessarily make you rich, but God will provide for your needs through it. Hard work will not necessarily make you famous, but it will give your witness authenticity.

Read the following Scriptures and create a motto for yourself about the work you do, whether at home or in a paying job. Proverbs 12:11,24; 13:14; 14:23; 21:5; 24:30-34.

Day 6 Greed

In the jungles of some of the most remote parts of the world there are large bands of monkeys. Their presence is revealed by a constant chatter in the branches far overhead. In the trees they are safe from the predators of the jungle floor and out of reach of human hunters desiring to take them captive.

The members of a number of jungle tribes have developed an elegant and simple trap which enables them to capture many monkeys for sale to zoos and institutions. They take a coconut and make a hole in it just large enough to accommodate the outstretched hand of the monkey, but too small to allow a clenched monkey fist to exit. A chain or piece of rope dangles from one end of the coconut. The cavity is filled with monkey bait such as grain or shiny objects.

The trapper goes into the jungle and locates a clutch of monkeys high in the trees. He holds up the coconut for the animals to see. It is a common object, so they show little interest. Then the hunter pours the contents of the coconut into his hand and holds it up for the monkeys to see. This action generates a great deal of excitement as the monkeys scramble to get a good view of the coveted items.

The trapper replaces the bait in the coconut, chains the trap to the base of a tree and walks into the jungle.

As soon as the human is a safe distance away the monkeys swarm to the trap. Generally the largest, fastest and greediest monkey will light upon the coconut, thrusting his hand into the opening and taking possession of the prize.

Discouraged, the other monkeys will stand around and wait for the victor to pull his prize out of the shell. But as the monkey tries to do so, he finds that he cannot pull his clenched fist through the opening. He has what he wants, but what he wants has him. To let go of the prize now would be unthinkable, for another monkey would snatch it. So the monkey will crouch in the forest with his hand clenched around his treasure until the hunter returns and takes him captive or until a wild beast devours him.

The creature is not held by the coconut. It is a passive trap. He is not held by the bait nor by the chain. He is held captive by one thing: his greed. We may laugh at the monkey for his foolishness, or we may learn from him.

Read the passages listed here and describe how greed might take you captive, what kind of bait you might be attracted to and how to avoid the trap. Proverbs 11:1; 13:11; 22:16; 28:8,24,25.

R.B., T.A.

Wisdom in the Family

Day 1 Who's in Charge

The tension on the football field was overwhelming. The coach was at it again—making more rules for conduct on the team. His team. The players had already been required to shave their heads (it makes a man look tough), they were forced to wear ties on game days (it makes the team look united), they were not allowed to be seen with girls (it might weaken their resolve), and now the coach was telling them that they had to be in bed by 10:00 every night. Many of the players began to ask themselves, "Who does this guy think he is, trying to run everybody's life?" The players wanted to play football, not to have their lives controlled by some fanatical ex-marine sergeant! Several of the best players quit in disgust. They wanted to have fun, and they didn't need someone else to tell them how to live. Those who stayed enjoyed the best season the team had had in years.

Authority. It's difficult to live under. It is everywhere, filling relationships with tension, bringing on disagreements, causing people to quit or rebel. Each individual wants personal control, to be able to do what he or she thinks is right at the right time.

Authority can be a big problem when living in the family. In the family, authority is spelled P-A-R-E-N-T-S. No matter what ideas people may have on how to face life, it seems as though their parents' ideas are different. One may want to watch TV at a friend's house, then study. The parents say study, then go to the friend's house. One may want to eat at 5:00. Parents say 6:00.

The battle with authority and who should have it never seems to end. Parents have an idea of what you should be like and you disagree. Even the color of the walls in your bedroom can become a battleground over the authority of parents and one's own independence.

Struggles with authority have gone on for thousands of years. While the struggle usually begins at home, the battle is fought for the length of one's life. Authority never goes away. There are never any easy answers for us when we are faced with the struggle over following authority. Proverbs tells us that our response to parental authority must be: "Listen to your father, who gave you life, and do not despise your mother when she is old" (23:22); "A wise son heeds his father's instruction, but a mocker does not listen to rebuke" (13:1). Living under the authority of parents is not always easy, but God has established them as a system to give definition and character to our lives. Listen to them, interact with them, respect the authority which has been given to them by God.

Read Romans 13:1-4. List all the people who have authority over you (parents, teachers, etc.).

How do you respond to each of them? Why?

According to verses 3 and 4, what is to be your response to authority?

Day 2 Disappointment

Tim was mad. His parents had done it to him again. They originally told him that he could go away for the weekend with his best friend, Tom. Then after all the plans were made and he was making his final preparations, his parents told him that they had reconsidered and they didn't want him to go. They never seemed to have good reasons for their actions and could never fully explain why they made the decisions they did. It appeared to Tim that every time he set up something fun for himself, his parents would not let him go ahead with his plans.

This time, he wasn't going to take it anymore. It wouldn't help to talk with them about it, they would just lecture. The only way Tim thought that he could get their attention was to work against them. He would quit doing his chores around the house. He would come home deliberately past the curfew that his parents set. He would refuse to talk with them at meal times—or any other time, for that matter.

Disappointment is a natural outgrowth of life in the family. If it's not the parents who disappoint, then it's brothers or sisters. Disappointment often becomes evident when we seem to have things ordered just as we'd like them, then someone messes our plans up!

Many times disappointment is handled the way Tim did it, with more hurt. Reactions to disappointments may bring about a refusal to cooperate, or an outburst of anger, or even a choice to stop communicating. Unfortunately, handling disappointment in that way usually deepens it rather than bringing relief.

Instead of unleashing a volley of harsh words when disappointed, "Through patience a ruler can be persuaded, and a gentle tongue can break a bone" (Prov. 25:15). Try a soft and gracious reply!

Practice listening to other family members and understanding what they are really saying: "Let the wise listen and add to their learning, and let the discerning get guidance" (Prov. 1:5).

Take a moment to think about a current (or recent) disappointment in your family. How have you responded to the person who disappointed you? What mistakes did you make? How can you make a wiser response to disappointments in the future?

Day 3 No Pain, No Gain

The book of Proverbs is full of wisdom. Within it is a great deal of practical advice on handling ourselves in life. Much of the wisdom is easy to apply—and the results are seen almost immediately. But some of the wisdom given is painful, and the results slow to become apparent. When reading statements concerning the wisdom of accepting discipline within the family, for instance, a person may quickly move on to another subject. Discipline is painful and hard to accept. Accepting discipline does not bring quick results. However, discipline does bring pain and struggle. Love brings happiness and peace. When discipline is evident, love is not apparent. Or so we think!

Proverbs 3:11,12 corrects that misconception. "My son, do not despise the Lord's discipline and do not rebuke, because the Lord disciplines those he loves, as a father the son he delights in." Punishment and discipline are proof of a father's love? Isn't that a little like junking a car because it gets good gas mileage? It just doesn't seem to make sense.

There was once a man who wanted to breed prize greyhounds to race. He wanted to have the best dogs around so he decided that his dogs would get the best care and love available. They ate only the choice cuts of meat. They lived in air conditioned kennels. They never had to exercise. They were pampered beyond the wildest of their dog dreams. They grew large (some might say plump!) from all of the attention and extra food they received. They grew lazy from underwork. The owner was proud.

Meanwhile, another man decided that he too would raise greyhounds for racing. He gave them quality high protein food—but not too much. He made them run every day even though at times they did not seem to enjoy it. His dogs became sleek, well-muscled, fast.

When the day of the first race came, the dogs who had had the "best" care, who had been able to eat as much as they wanted, who had never run, were not even able to move beyond the starting line. They just acted as they usually did— very sleepy!

The other dogs, however, who were forced to run every

day and had a reasonable diet, became famous for their speed.

Which owner loved his dogs more? The one who gave them everything they desired or the one who gave them only what he knew was important for their livelihood?

Proverbs contains these instructions for parents: "Do not withhold discipline from a child; if you punish him with the rod, he will not die" and "Discipline your son, for in that there is hope; do not be a willing party to his death" (Prov. 23:13; 19:18).

The wise family is the one that disciplines and accepts discipline as an important means of exercising love and developing abilities to cope with life.

Read Proverbs 19:18 and 23:13. Why is discipline connected with death in these verses?

Read Ephesians 6:1-4. What is promised to those who follow the discipline of their parents?

How do you profit from your parents' discipline?

What does it mean to "honor" your parents?

Day 4 Life in Parloma

Parloma is a tiny nation which lies approximately thirteen miles south and four miles west of Bird City, Kansas. The people of this unique land are different only in that they seem to lack any true understanding of how to go about the tasks of living. Personal relationships are almost nonexistent. Each person spends time daily in searching for necessities such as food, water, and shelter. There is little conversation and even less laughter. Skills are primitive at best.

Sociologists, curious about the habits of the people, studied this strange culture and made a startling discovery: In Parloma there are no families! Upon birth, each individual is left alone to discover life. Among Parlomians this fact is a cause for happiness, for there is no one to demand obedience and each can do as he or she pleases. But some of the more intelligent Parlomians have begun to realize that not having families is a problem. No one learns how to relate to others because the people have never seen anyone else do it. No one learns crafts with which to make a living because there is no one who can teach. No one knows about love and understanding. The character of the people is lacking because there is no one to correct, to direct, to support, to love. So all the people do what they think is right and have found themselves caught in a life of boredom and directionlessness.

Proverbs, the book of wisdom, contains illustrations of the character-building process that occurs in families. "My son, do not despise the Lord's discipline and do not resent his rebuke, because the Lord disciplines those he loves, as a father the son he delights in." (3:11,12). Families, especially parents, have been given the responsibility to develop our abilities to be relational people, to choose values, to learn responsibility. Without the influence of the family, a person's life would lack stability and direction. "The way of a fool is right in his own eyes, but a wise man is he who listens to counsel" (12:15).

The family has been established by God to build a proper outlook on life that is able to stand up to the pressures of living in our world. We are all stamped with the likeness of our family—that is what makes us unique!

Read Deuteronomy 6:5-9. What is the greatest influence on character a family has?

How can you be involved in the character-shaping process in your family?

Day 5 The Most Difficult Word

"Children, obey your parents in the Lord, for this is right. 'Honor your father and mother'—which is the first commandment with a promise—'that it may go well with you and that you may enjoy long life on the earth' " (Eph. 6:1-3). "Obedience" is a hard word for people to get used to. When one thinks of what it means to obey, thoughts of slavery and a loss of freedom seem to come. Many individuals fight hard against the idea of obedience to parents almost from the day they are born.

Author Sheldon Vanauken describes the reason and need for obedience with a story about a dog and a rabbit.

Gypsy was a furry and comfortable-looking collie who lived on several hundred acres of land—pure dog paradise. There were rabbit trails to explore and streams to ford. In short, virtually everything a dog could delight in was available to her. Her only real obligation was to worship and obey her master. She knew that she must not chase the chickens, and must obey certain basic commands such as to follow, to come, to lie down.

One day when Gypsy was doing her usual running around, two things happened at once. The master called her and a rabbit fled across the hill. Her first instinct was to obey her master, but she stopped in her tracks as the thought entered her mind that she didn't have to obey. Perhaps the master didn't really understand about the rabbit. She was a free dog and she chose to chase the rabbit as the master called for her once again.

After hours of chasing the rabbit, Gypsy came home. Rather than approaching the master with joy as she had before, she guiltily crept toward him, pleading for forgiveness. She was obedient for several days, but later there was another rabbit and this time she did not even hesitate, she ran as the master called for her. Soon, the mere thought of a rabbit would send her racing off into the hills.

The master still loved her but no longer trusted her. In time she lived in a pen and went for walks with a rope around her neck. All her real freedom was gone. Occasionally she was given a chance to obey. Had she chosen to obey she would once again have had perfect freedom to wander about the acres. But she did not return to the obedience. Her freedom was taken from her and her life became tedious, boring, restrained. (From: *A Severe Mercy.* Harper & Row, Publishers, Inc., New York, 1977.)

Proverbs explains that the instructions of our parents are given to aid us as we develop as independent individuals who are able to respond to the crises which reach us every day (see Prov. 12:5; 3:11,12; 13:1). Parents attempt in love to guide each person to a better understanding of life and the challenges which lie ahead. Freedom is built upon a foundation of obedience; disobedience brings a faulty character and a damaged ability to respond to the challenges of life. You are free to choose: disobedience and struggle or obedience and freedom.

Read Proverbs 5:12–14. Have these words ever been yours?

Read Ephesians 6:1–4 and Colossians 3:20,21. What does the promise "that it may go well with you and that you may enjoy long life on the earth" mean?

Think of one area of your life where you are not obedient. Ask for God's power to change so that you can grow!

Day 6 To Kill a Dragon

A hungry tramp wandered into a small village one day looking for a handout. He came upon a tiny inn and decided to try his luck at begging for food. He knocked upon the door and a rather harried-looking cook opened. She looked contemptuously at the man's tattered clothes and dirty appearance. After the old man had made his plea for some food, the cook angrily replied: "You are a no-good bum who is lazy and dirty and probably a thief. I would never give you even one bite of food. Get a job and work for your food like everyone else." She then harshly slammed the door in his face. Dejected, the man turned and began to walk away. When he was halfway up the street, he turned to gaze one last time at the inn. He noticed a sign at the front of the inn, stating the name The Inn of St. George and the Dragon. Excited by a sudden inspiration, he walked quickly back to the inn and once again knocked upon the door. When the cook appeared, he asked, "May I speak to St. George this time?"

Individuals often act out the dual characters of St. George and the dragon within the family. When a good impression is to be made, St. George's peaceful and kind characteristics come forth. But at other times the gruff and angry personality of the dragon (fiery breath and all!) is demonstrated. There are memories of hurt which create an atmosphere of tension among family members which give rise to dragon-like anger. There are fresh quarrels over issues that never seem to be resolved. The dragon feeds on a lack of forgiveness toward other family members. When anger, pain, or grudges are not driven away by the force of forgiveness, the dragon of bitterness becomes stronger and stronger, even consuming the person in which it lives.

Forgiveness toward the people who have offended us is the only way to contain and destroy that powerful dragon that can live within. Colossians 3:13 instructs us to "Bear with each other and forgive whatever grievances you may have against one another. Forgive as the Lord forgave you." You must choose to kill the dragon by applying the same forgiveness which Christ freely gives to you.

But how can we forgive those other members in our family

who seem to know how to offend us without even trying? One way is to be aware that the wisdom of other family members is needed and helpful: "The way of a fool is right in his own eyes, but a wise man is he who listens to counsel" (Prov. 12:15). Another is to apply patience: "A man's wisdom gives him patience; it is to his glory to overlook an offense" (Prov. 19:11).

Most importantly, love is to surround life in the family—not merely speaking about love, but actually practicing it (see 1 John 3:18).

The dragon of bitter unforgiveness will raise its ugly head when the wisdom of Proverbs is not applied to life in the family. When disagreement, disappointment, misunderstanding, or anger come along, kill the dragon by practicing the wisdom of forgiveness. Be a dragonslayer!

Think about everything you haven't forgiven a family member. Make a list of those things on a sheet of paper.

Read Luke 17:3,4. To what extent does Jesus command us to forgive?

Read Matthew 18:21-35. What are the consequences when you do not forgive? (See v. 35.) Does Jesus put any qualifications on forgiveness? According to verse 35, where does forgiveness start?

Look at your list of grievances against fellow family members. Do you choose to forgive them? If so, tear up the list and throw it away. You've just killed a dragon!

B.B.

Wisdom with Friends

Day 1 The Importance of Friends

One of the most tragic stories of our time came to an end when a man was found dead in his hotel room. At the time he was found, his physical appearance was so strange that those who once knew him would not have been able to recognize him. He had a straggly beard that hung down to his waist, and his greasy hair reached the middle of his back. His fingernails were more than two inches long, and his toenails were so long that he could no longer wear shoes. It is hard to believe that at one time he was married to one of the most beautiful women in the world.

This man had spent the last few years of his life shuffling from one resort hotel to another. Each time when he would arrive, he would order the windows shut, the curtains drawn and the doors locked so that he could be alone in the dark while he watched the same old movie over and over again, until the day he died. Howard Hughes was one of the richest and most powerful men in the world. He had the money and the power to get whatever he wanted, yet he chose to live the life of a lunatic, in isolation from the rest of the world.

We may never know the reason why Howard Hughes's life ended the way it did, but we do know that his life lacked one important element: he had no friends.

Friends are important for all of us, regardless of how much or how little we have materially. No matter how independent we would like to be, we all need people with whom we can share our lives, people who love us for who we really are. God often uses special people in our lives to teach us, correct us or comfort us. Those people are usually our friends, or at least they should be. The Bible has a lot to say about friendships, and it is no surprise that a book about wisdom has some good advice for us. Here's a great piece of advice from Proverbs 13:20: "He who walks with the wise grows wise, but a companion of fools suffers harm." It's no secret that we tend to become like the people we hang around with. Paul stated the same idea in 1 Corinthians 15:33. Proverbs is saying that if we want to be wise, we had better have wise friends.

Choosing good friends is important for a lot of reasons. Many times we just want someone to talk with, or someone to give us some advice when we need it. Proverbs 27:9 says, "Oil and perfume make the heart glad, so a man's counsel is sweet to his friend."

Think of the people in your life who are your closest friends. How do you feel when you spend time talking with them about the things that are important to you?

Do these people know that they are important to you?

Have you ever thanked them for being your friends? Think of some ways in which you could do that, and tell your friends how you feel about them today.

Day 2 Unconditional Love

During World War I, two young men who had been friends since their early childhood found themselves fighting in the same area of battle. They had grown up together playing, studying and competing side by side, and now here they were again, side by side in combat.

One day after a long and dangerous battle, it was discovered that one of the soldiers was missing. The other, who had returned from the battle safe and unharmed, went to the commanding officer and asked permission to go out and look for his friend. The officer told him it was no use, that no one could still be alive in that battlefield. But after strong pleading by the young man, the officer finally gave him permission to go. Several hours later he returned with the limp body of his friend over his shoulder.

"Didn't I tell you it was no use to go?" asked the commanding officer.

"But it was not," the soldier responded with radiance in his eyes. "I got there in time to hear him whisper, 'I knew you'd come.'"

All of us would like to have a friend like that, a friend who would watch out for us and care for us, a friend who would love us when everyone else had turned their backs on us. Proverbs gives a great definition of a friend: "A friend loves at all times" (Prov. 17:17). Unfortunately, that's not true of most people. A friend who loves at all times is rare. Many people love other people because of something: because of how much money they have; because of who their friends are;

because of what they can do for others. Proverbs 19:6 says, "Everyone is the friend of a man who gives gifts." That's why celebrities, politicians, and entertainers are often very lonely people. They have no real friends, only people who love them because of what they can do for them.

The Bible talks about a different kind of love, a love that says, "I love you in spite of" . . . in spite of the fact that you have no money, in spite of the way you dress, in spite of how other people feel about you. That's real love, and that's what real friendship is all about. Proverbs 18:24 says, "A man of many friends comes to ruin, but there is a friend who sticks closer than a brother." In other words, it's not how many friends you have, it's the quality of those friendships that counts. Do you have friends who love you with "because of" love, or with "in spite of" love?

That unconditional "in spite of" love is one of the marks of a true and lasting friendship. Take a look at 1 Corinthians 13:4-8: These are the qualities of "in spite of" love. Read through the passage again, and this time say your name instead of the word "love" when you read the verse. Are those things true about you? Make a list of the qualities you need to work on, and think of a way you could grow in that area by showing that kind of love to a friend today.

Day 3 Being a Faithful Friend

The people in our country were shocked to learn that a great deal of our most top-secret military information was recently sold to a communist government by an American citizen. Lured by the promise of big money and the excitement of international intrigue, he sold out. The price of betraying his country is high: he will be tried on several counts of treason and will face the possibility of a life sentence. Fifty years ago, he would have had to face a firing squad.

Treason, betrayal, disloyalty: these are strong words that we hope are never applied to us. But here's something to think about—what's the difference between betraying the confidence of a country and betraying the confidence of a friend? How many times have you said or heard these lines: "Debbie asked me not to tell anybody, but I know that I can trust you. Anyway, here's what she said . . . " "Do you know what Dave told me about him? Not many people know about this, but Kim told me . . . "

It's true that when people are good friends, they share secrets with each other. They tell things to each other that they would never say to someone else. There is nothing wrong with telling your own secrets to a friend, but remember that secrets give one person power over another. A true friend is one who knows how to keep a secret. Proverbs 11:13 says, "A gossip betrays a confidence, but a trustworthy man keeps a secret." When you tell a friend something, you are not just giving information, you are putting trust and confidence in that person. You believe that he or she is going to keep your secret. True friends are loyal no matter what the cost. They refuse to cut you down or give away your secrets. You will know your true friends because of their uncompromising loyalty. The book of Proverbs gives some strong advice about giving away secrets. Anyone who is wise knows that gossiping and slandering are sure ways to lose friends. Read the following verses and write down the advice each one gives to you:

Proverbs 10:19: "When words are many, sin is not absent, but he who holds his tongue is wise."

Proverbs 16:28: "A perverse man stirs up dissension, and a gossip separates close friends."

Proverbs 17:9: "He who covers over an offense promotes love, but whoever repeats the matter separates close friends."

Proverbs 20:19: "A gossip betrays a confidence; so avoid a man who talks too much."

What should you do if you find yourself starting to gossip? Try to memorize this little prayer from Psalm 141:3: "Set a guard over my mouth; O Lord, keep watch over the door of my lips."

Day 4 Being Honest with a Friend

"The Emperor's New Clothes" is a story by Hans Christian Andersen about an emperor who was so fond of clothes that he spent all his time and money in order to be well dressed. One day two very clever men came to the emperor and told him they were weavers who could make the emperor a set of clothes from magic cloth. They told the emperor that this magic cloth could not be seen by anyone who was unfit for his or her office or anyone who was very stupid.

The emperor was intrigued by this idea, so he gave the weavers a large amount of money to make him a set of clothes from this magic cloth. For many days, the two men pretended to be weaving this magic cloth, and when the emperor sent his officers to examine their work, none of them would admit they could not see the cloth, for they were afraid that the emperor would have them removed from office.

On the day the clothes were to be ready, the emperor ordered a great procession in which he would be able to show off his new clothes as he marched through the town. The day came and the two men came with the emperor's clothes, which were really nothing at all. They pretended to dress the emperor while his officers complimented him on how splendid he looked in his new royal robes. The emperor then went off to show off his new clothes.

As he walked through the town, the people were afraid to say that the emperor had no clothes on. A little boy who was watching the procession shouted out, "But the king has nothing on at all!" At that point, everyone knew the boy had told the truth, and the people laughed at the emperor as he continued his procession through the town.

The story of the emperor's new clothes shows us an important truth about friendship. What good are friends who won't tell you the truth? Proverbs puts it this way: "Faithful are the wounds of a friend, but deceitful are the kisses of an enemy" (27:6). While on the one hand we should love and accept our friends, that does not mean we have to approve of everything they do or think. Sometimes we need to give some constructive criticism with love and patience. Receiving those constructive criticisms can sometimes be painful. That's why Proverbs calls them "wounds." But because we give them in love, we can say that wounds are faithful.

We need to be careful of those people who tell us only good things or only what we want to hear. Ben Franklin used to say, "The same cannot be both friend and flatterer." Many times those people want to get something from us, so they set a trap with their words. Proverbs 29:5 says, "Whoever flatters his neighbor is spreading a net for his feet." All of us like to be praised, admired and looked up to, but that's not always the best thing for us. We sometimes need to be confronted with our weaknesses, so that we can grow. Friends that conceal things from us don't do us any favors.

King David was a powerful but also a popular king. When he committed adultery with Bathsheba, and then made arrangements so that her husband would be killed, no one wanted to tell David he was wrong. A man who would do those things would surely kill the one who stood in front of him.

Nathan was a prophet, but he was also David's friend. He loved David and he was not afraid to confront him. Because Nathan corrected him, David humbled himself before God and was forgiven. Who knows what would have happened if Nathan had not loved David enough to confront him? Proverbs 28:23 says, "He who rebukes a man will in the end gain more favor than he who has a flattering tongue." Nathan's action demonstrated the truth of that statement. Do you have anyone in your life who will correct you in love when you are wrong?

Have you ever asked someone to keep an eye on you and help you to grow? Think of someone who will help you do this, and talk to him or her about it.

Day 5 Are You a Menace?

One of the most popular comics in almost every newspaper in the country is Dennis the Menace. Dennis is a mischievous boy with a lot of energy who is always getting into trouble. Dennis has a friend who lives next door—Mr. Wilson, who is old enough to be Dennis's grandfather. Dennis likes to go over to Mr. Wilson's house, and he does so about once a day. Mrs. Wilson likes to have Dennis come over, but Mr. Wilson would just as soon have Dennis stay on his own side of the fence. Every time Dennis comes over, he gets into trouble with Mr. Wilson for something, and Mr. Wilson ends up chasing him out of the house. It's not that Mr. Wilson is a mean old man, it's that Dennis is a menace. One of the definitions that Webster gives for a menace is "a person who causes annoyance."

Maybe you know a few menaces. All of us know people who get on our nerves after a while. They are nice people and we like them, but sometimes they do things that make it hard for us to be around them. Did you ever think that maybe you sometimes get on the nerves of others?

The book of Proverbs gives great advice on things to do to make our friendships better. It also gives great advice on some things to avoid in order to be better friends. Proverbs 25:17 says, "Seldom set foot in your neighbor's house—too much of you, and he will hate you."

There are a couple of ways that we sometimes try to take up too much of our friends. One way is wanting always to be around them at school, at home, at practice, on weekends, and so on. You can avoid this by giving your friends time and space to do what they choose without you. Another way we take up too much of our friends is by being jealous or possessive about their friendship. Sometimes we want to be a person's best friend or *only* friend. Jealousy or possessiveness can rise up and strangle friendships just as weeds strangle flowers. Give your friends the freedom to have other friends and the right to be with other people. Your own friendships will be stronger because of it.

Another piece of advice comes from Proverbs 27:14: "If a man loudly blesses his neighbor early in the morning, it will be taken as a curse." Another way to put this is, if you call your friend up at 2 A.M. to say you hope he or she is having a good night's sleep, he or she may not get the message you intend. Insensitivity causes friction in any friendship. Be careful not to do things that bother those around you, especially those you really care for.

Another thing to watch out for comes from Proverbs 26:18,19: "Like a madman shooting firebrands or deadly arrows is a man who deceives his neighbor and says, 'I was only joking.'" Have you ever had your feelings hurt by a person who then said, "I was only kidding"? It probably didn't make you feel any better. Be careful that you don't make jokes at another person's expense. If everyone can't laugh at your joke, then it is not worth it.

Another thing to watch out for is inappropriate cheerfulness. "Like one who takes away a garment on a cold day, or like vinegar poured on soda, is one who sings songs to a heavy heart" (Prov. 25:20). Sometimes we get so wrapped up in ourselves that we fail to think about anyone else. The remedy is to be thoughtful, to think of others.

What are some other things that destroy friendships that we should avoid? List five things.

Read Hebrews 10:24. What are some things that you could do to encourage your friends to love one another and do good deeds? List five things.

Day 6 Traits of a True Friend

One of the greatest gifts God has given to us is friendship with others. There is tremendous joy in having and being a friend. God knew that there would be times when we would need people in our lives to love us and care for us and share our joys and sorrows. A friend is someone who knows us well, but loves us anyway.

God also knows that it is good for us to reach out to others when they are in need. Sometimes it forces us to think of others' needs and put them ahead of our own as we love, care, and share. That's what friendship is all about.

One of the most beautiful love stories in the Bible is that of two friends, David and Jonathan. David was a young shepherd boy who volunteered to fight the Philistine warrior, Goliath, who had been terrorizing the army of Israel. David killed Goliath with a stone from his sling and became a national hero. King Saul summoned David, and at that meeting David met Jonathan, the king's son. And there they became instant friends.

Read 1 Samuel 18:1-4. How does the Bible say Jonathan loved David? What did Jonathan do for David?

Read 1 Samuel 18:5-9. When Saul saw how David was gaining popularity with the people, he became jealous and violent. On two occasions, Saul tried to kill David by hurling a spear at him. On several other occasions, he set traps for him or sent him on difficult missions, hoping that David might be killed. If David was killed, Jonathan would have been the most likely candidate to replace Saul as king. Do you think David trusted Jonathan? Would you have trusted him? Read 1 Samuel 19:1-7. In defending David, Jonathan stood up to his father and reminded Saul of all the good that David had done. What are the qualities you see in Jonathan here?

Saul's jealousy and hatred toward David soon returned and David was forced to leave the palace. Jonathan and David met together in secret and formed a plan to determine how angry Saul really was. Read 1 Samuel 20:30-42. What did Jonathan do again for David? What were the consequences? Is it always easy to stick up for a friend? Why did David and Jonathan cry? What was responsible for their commitment to each other?

David began to live the life of a nomad, always staying one step ahead of Saul, who was still trying to kill him. After a while, David became discouraged. He was tired of running for his life. Jonathan went to David and encouraged him. Read 1 Samuel 23:15-18. What was the news that Jonathan gave to David? What did that mean for David? What did that mean for Jonathan? How do you think Jonathan saw David in relationship to himself?

Saul continued to pursue David so hard that David had to flee from his own country. Saul eventually was killed in a battle with the Philistines, which ended Saul's threat on David's life. While David could have rejoiced, he mourned over the loss of his king. He also mourned because his friend, Jonathan, was killed in the same battle. David composed a sad poem over the death of Jonathan. Read it in 2 Samuel 1:25-27. How did David describe Jonathan's love for him? How would someone describe your love for him or her?

Take a minute to think back over the story of David and Jonathan. What things made their relationship so special? Two of the things they did were to spend time and effort in developing their friendship. Good friendships don't happen overnight. They take time. Time to care, time to share, time to

love. Good friendships also take effort: doing things for those
who are important to you, making sacrifices to put the other
person ahead of yourself. Remember that to have friends, you
must first be a friend; the quality of friends you have will be
determined by the quality of friend you are.

T.A.

The Wisdom
of Self-Discipline

Day 1 Put Your Muscle Where Your Heart Is

"Surfers don't have any self-discipline," the minister said. Those words always cut into me. I have been a waterbug ever since I can remember. At the age of eleven I started sluggin' it out with the sea for a chance to ride her emerald arms back to the beach. But here I was sitting in church being told that I didn't have any self-discipline . . . and that our whole breed didn't have any self-discipline. On the surface it seemed to be true.

The minister used football players as a contrast. They endured tight control, countless sit-ups and endless days of aching muscles. They were team players. They attended school, they attended games (naturally), and many had fairly good grades. They tended to be prompt, tight and very "together"—all for the privilege of chasing an inflated pigskin across a clump of grass.

We surf rats were different. We were flaky, undependable, truant, often uninterested in the affairs of school. We seldom got to the games and had a tendency to fall asleep in class. As we drifted off from high school those of us who held onto the sport seemed to acquire jobs that had no long-term goals or that we could manipulate to accommodate our life-style.

It came as a refreshing revelation to realize one sunny day while sitting on the beach that we were not a bunch of slouches but that we were actually a highly-disciplined group of individuals. You see, surfers' life-styles are dictated by the patterns of the waves and the weather. These are very unpredictable. To be a good surfer means to be constantly in touch with the elements and when they produce good surf to forsake everything to go surfing. Surfers are disciplined to the dictates of the sport.

Since our sport demands that we be able to expend the time and energy when conditions are right, we may be truant when the swell is up. We may take on jobs that we can wrap around the discipline of our sport. We get up at the crack of dawn and patrol the beaches hoping that the night has produce a perfect south swell. We surf until it is dark and our stomachs howl with hunger. We paddle out in freezing cold water just because the waves are good. We risk sharks and coral because we are disciplined to our sport.

We humans will discipline ourselves to something that we love. We will obey its commands without much hesitation. Ask any mountain climber, athlete or craftsman. They spend the time in discipline because they love what they are doing.

Galatians 5:22,23 tells us of the natural overflow that comes from a person who loves Jesus Christ. It is called the fruit of the Spirit. One of the traits listed is self-control. It comes as a natural part of life when we are growing in Christ and living for Him.

1. Read 1 Corinthians 9:24-27 and compare the self-discipline of an athlete with your self-discipline in various areas by making a chart showing what a typical athlete must do to stay in physical shape and what a Christian must do to stay in spiritual shape.
2. Chart your physical and spiritual progress on the chart for this next week.

Day 2 The Self-Disciplined Stomach

There are certain topics that are "hot potatoes" for any minister to take up. One such subject is an area of self-control that has been neglected by both congregation and clergy alike. It can't be discussed tactfully because its violators have tipped their hands already. They are ready-made targets as they sit in their pews with the evidence of their guilt literally hanging on them. They are gluttons.

Such an ugly word. The vision you see is of a slobbering, gross pig-person greasing his or her face with a turkey leg. Surely there are no gluttons in our midst! Perhaps the biblical injunction against gluttony is a cultural teaching, aimed at the decadent Romans who used to gorge themselves with food and then throw up so they could eat some more. Even their sculpture shows that they thought "meat on the bones" was a sign of beauty. Now those people were gluttons!

Sorry—even though the word "glutton" means "an eater" in the Greek, its connotation is almost always one who eats without control.

Our society is very conscious of weight. Diets are begun and abandoned by the millions every day in the hope of attaining some sort of resemblance to the models in the magazines. We are against overeating not so much because it is a sign of poor self-control but because it is not the way to achieve the look of today. If the fashion in body types should change (they do that from time to time, you know) and the desirable body style should become "chunky," affluent western-world people would probably cram even more food into their mouths than they do already.

Gluttony is eating without self-control. It should not be that hard to figure out when we are full and then simply stop eating. But we have the luxury (not shared by the majority of the world) to be able to "top our tanks"—and we do so in ever-increasing amounts.

Perhaps we had better take a clue from the book of Proverbs and see that this form of self-abuse leads to poverty. There is poverty of body: for each extra pound we carry we pay a price in terms of longevity, health and vitality. There is poverty of example: what kind of example is a fat, flabby body? And there is poverty of compassion. Compassion? We buy what we don't need, eat what we aren't hungry for, and throw away piles of food. With a little planning and conservation we might be able to use that extra dollar that we are "eating" needlessly for those who need to eat.

Read Proverbs 23:19-21. Write a manifesto that you need to follow when it comes to self-control and food.

Day 3 The Self-Control to Stick to It

The trip had been planned for months. It took more than eight hours to arrive at the foothills of the majestic Sierra Nevada mountain range. It would take two more before we reached our starting point of 8,000 feet. There were ten of us, including the youth pastor and his wife. We were loaded down with our packs, tents, bedrolls and dehydrated food. We were confident that we would make this Sierra trek the best one ever. The boys in the party generously offered to help some of the girls by carrying the heavier loads. We spent the night at a lower level to acclimatize ourselves.

The next day we began the ascent. We had hiked for only about a quarter of a mile from our base camp when one of the girls began to drag behind. Most of us were fresh with energy and anticipation, so we left her to straggle in the rear with a close friend and the youth pastor. (His wife was leading the hike at a faster pace than most of us wanted to maintain!)

By a half mile out the slowpoke refused to go any further. We were getting steamed, but we went back to take some more of her load. She tried again, but a few hundred yards further down the trail she sat down and confessed to having asthma. She hadn't admitted it earlier because she was afraid she would not be allowed to go on the trip. The group stripped her of all her gear. She had plenty of medication and was in no actual danger. She simply had not become accustomed to the altitude as quickly as the rest of us. We had to coax her one step at a time to keep on going.

The trip would have been called off if she had not been willing to push on. It was not fun—not for her nor for the rest of us waiting at each turn and rise. But she pushed on, one step after another. Someone got her a walking stick, someone walked with her at each step of the path, and we all carried her load. But *she* determined the outcome of that hike.

We finally got to our first campsite, and by morning our friend had regained her wind and was hauling herself and her gear up the trail with the rest of us.

The point to all of this is simple. Getting somewhere in the spiritual realm is not always easy. The climate may not be what you are used to. While you don't have to bear all of the burdens yourself, it is up to your own self-control to keep plodding along. The members of the Body of Christ need you to do that. They will help you if you let them know that you are struggling (preferably before you are totally out of wind). They will carry what they can, but you have to carry yourself. This does not mean that you have to pull yourself up by your boot-straps and become some sort of spiritual mountain leaper. It does mean that you press on the best you can in watching your tongue, controlling your physical drives, doing what needs to be done to nourish yourself through prayer and Bible study. Ultimately the Body of Christ needs you to carry on and not give up. Push the limits of self-discipline; you'll be surprised at how far you can go. You might even find a strength you never knew you had.

Read Isaiah 40:28-31. What kind of encouragement does this passage give you in your quest for a self-disciplined life?

Day 4 Self-Disciplined Communications

Those of us who set about to become transformed by the Spirit living within us have a sad awakening sooner or later when we discover that the completely self-disciplined life is not to be found this side of eternity.

Just when we think that we have some major section of our life under submission another blemish of the soul seems to break through. (Probably the new problem was there all along but our awareness of it was dulled by other preoccupations.)

Perhaps no single area is more typical of the problem just described than that of communication. James recommended that we bridle our tongues (see Jas. 3:1-12). Jesus said that our speech betrays our inner heart (see Matt. 12:34). The words that come out of our mouths are often vile and ugly. At other times our words are mistimed, misspoken and just plain stupid.

Take a moment to recall the last time you wished that you hadn't said something. It probably wasn't so long ago. Oh, to have a mouth that was wired shut! Not only would you lose weight, you would have to make sure that what you were going to say was worth the effort of squirting it out past clenched teeth.

There are proverbs and sayings to fill many a volume on the subject of ill-used speech, but what is the source of the problem? For slander, gossip, lie-spreading and other forms of malicious talk it is the heart condition that must bear the blame. But for the foolish statement, the poorly timed joke, and the clumsy attempt at being relevant, interesting or cute there is little to blame but a lack of self-control.

It would be wonderful to be able to say that there are a few basic steps to cure this malady—a formula to follow, certain prayers to say—but it isn't true. The sad fact is that the great majority of us (in fact, probably all of us) can improve but we cannot become perfect. (Note that even mute people communicate—if not with words, with that equally betraying device, the face.)

We can load our minds with advice such as, "It is better to be silent and be thought a fool than to open your mouth and remove all doubt" (see Prov. 17:27,28). We can ingest countless Scripture passages. These may all help, but they will not finally tame the tongue.

Then what is the point of trying? Well, ultimately because you will be a fool less often. Twenty years from now you may have the same uneasy feeling that you have just inserted your foot into your mouth, but the feeling may come less often and the foot may not be inserted as far.

It is true that learning self-discipline is a lot of work. It is true that spontaneous eruptions can prove delightful and humorous while well-thought-out dialogue can seem wooden and stilted. But it is also true that a lack of careful consideration of the impact of our words has put many of us in extremely uncomfortable situations. Wooden speech would have been preferable to what we actually said.

Read Proverbs 18:4. Give an example of deep thinking as expressed in speech.

Give the same idea as it might be expressed in shallow or thoughtless speech.

Think about how a stream gets deep. What does that tell you about the practice of self-discipline in the area of speech?

Day 5 Sexual Self-Control

There is an image painted in the pages of Proverbs that seems to come from the back alleys of some grimy Hollywood neighborhood. It is the picture of a sultry temptress who lures her victims into a trap that affords pleasure only for a moment. (See Prov. 5:1-23.) The reality of sexual temptation has not changed with the ages. Neither has the fact that God wants us to have self-discipline in every area of life, including the area of sex.

Many people find the self-discipline to do some extremely difficult things, but not to exercise sexual self-control.

A recent poll of single Protestant Christians showed that most believe that people should not be sexually active outside of marriage. However, 40 percent of those responding to the poll admitted that they had had premarital intercourse at least once.

There seems to be a problem—not with knowing God's will, but with doing God's will.

Anyone who has felt the tug of physical passion knows that the fight is not easy. We Christians are surrounded by people caught up in the popular myth that our bodies' passions and desires must be permitted to rule. We can feel left out, alone and even "puritanical" as we cling to our principles while people around us—even some Christians—do not follow the Lord's commands in their sexual activities.

When we know that sex is not inherently wrong (it isn't) . . . when we know that obeying God means no sexual intercourse until the conditions are right in God's eyes (that is, marriage) . . . when we know that an unknown span of years may pass before those conditions are right . . . we can get discouraged. Our self-control can be crushed and finally defeated.

But there are some things we can do to strengthen and encourage our self-discipline. Here are some of them.

First, don't feed the fire. The more sexually-oriented mental stimulation you allow yourself to have, the more difficulty you will have in controlling your thoughts. Involve your mind in creative and intelligent pursuits. Avoid the junk that stokes the furnace.

Second, discover the "love" of your life as a *person,* not as a body. Set yourself up to win rather than to fail. Spend time discovering the personality and character of the other person before you start exchanging your chewing gum.

Third, think about creative ways to be "semi-private." You don't want others around to hear your private conversation of love—but privacy is not necessarily total solitude. It can help you keep a lid on your own desires when there are people strolling by occasionally.

Fourth, make creative times happen—don't expect them to happen on their own. People who date for sexual conquest go to great lengths to plan for a sexual encounter—the right place, the right mood music, every detail planned in advance for the sake of seduction. Yet others who are looking forward to spending time with a person they care about often do not know how to plan that time in a way that will make it easier to stick to God-given principles. Do some advance thinking about ways to have a good time without exposing yourselves to too-tempting situations.

Fifth, be up front about your value system. It may shock

some people, but it makes it clear where you stand.

For the problems that come from losing a grip on sexual self-discipline, review Proverbs 5:1-23. And if you think that the need for sexual self-discipline ends entirely when you say "I do," think again. If you can't control the small beast now it may become a monster later.

Day 6 Out of Self-Control

Skateboarding is a sport that seems to have cycles of popularity like hula-hoops and yo-yos. When the popularity of skateboarding gets into full swing it is not unusual to see every street infested with slaloming daredevils. It also seems that every neighborhood has an incline to master—a feat that serves as a sort of "rite of manhood" in the skateboard world.

Jim was a new convert to skateboarding. He begged a ride to the top of a mile-long grade that began with deceptive gentleness and then pitched downward toward a climax at the end of the street. The guys at the top were hard-core veterans. They had paid their dues by bouncing along the asphalt. They now wore helmets, knee pads, gloves and other protective gear. Jim showed up in jeans, a t-shirt and tennis shoes. "Are you sure you are going to be able to do this?" one of the pros asked.

"Sure, no sweat," Jim replied. He pushed off and began to cut back and forth across the street, trying to control the velocity of his descent. Someone pulled a small movie camera out of a daypack and recorded the chain of events for posterity.

Jim began to pick up speed, but he still felt in control of the little board under his feet. The houses began to blur as Jim swept by them. The skateboard grew uneasy under his feet. He tried to guide it into a controlled turn to slow the speed, but the wheels began to slide. Jim quickly straightened out again, not wanting to risk a spill. Faster and faster he went—thirty miles per hour, then thirty-five. It seemed as though things were suddenly not as much in control as he had hoped they would be—and he still had the steepest descent in front of him. Jim wondered if he should bail out now and take his chances with the pavement, but he thought that he still had just enough control to make it.

The camera recorded the following sequence. Jim's board began to rock, slowly at first and then faster and faster until it pitched under his feet. Jim flipped off the skateboard at about forty miles per hour. The cameraman pressed the slow-motion button and recorded a roll, a flip off of one knee and then a ten-foot slide followed by the scarlet color of skinned flesh. Jim had lost control. There was a point when he could have turned back, a point where he might have bailed out, and a point after which there was nothing he could do to regain control.

Jim crawled into the car of a friend who would take him home to nurse his wounds. As he slid painfully into the back seat a couple of little guys came marching up the hill, new skateboards in hand. Jim leaned out of the window and said, "Hey, guys, it's a pretty tough hill."

The smallest one replied, "Aw, we can handle it."

There may be nothing unusual about the true story just related. Just another kid out of control, past his limits, biting the concrete. Maybe that's why the apostle Paul reminded Titus that self-control is a virtue for young and old alike. Maybe he knew something about the human spirit being out of control. Maybe he had a little insight that we could apply to everyday living.

Read Titus 2:1-15. Make a list of all the things that followers of Christ should show as part of their character. How many times is self-control listed there?

R.B.

Wisdom in Our Witness

Day 1 Does Wisdom Witness?

What picture does wisdom bring to your mind? Do you envision a quiet owl perched in a tree or a sage old man combing his beard? Or do you picture a smart-alecky younger brother making wisecracks? What does a wise person look like?

As the writer of Proverbs stated the purpose for writing his book, he mentioned several outward signs of wisdom: "a disciplined and prudent life, doing what is right and just and fair" (Prov. 1:3). Wisdom exceeds knowing and understanding—it fosters action. As we grow in understanding, our lives reflect what is "right and just and fair" even in situations where no rules exist. Wisdom helps us weigh the pros and cons and make just and right decisions. A wise person knows what to do, what to expect and how to treat people. Others notice and listen to wise people because their uncommonly good judgment makes them stand out.

King Solomon realized his inability to govern Israel, so he asked for a discerning heart (see 1 Kings 3:7-9). God granted his request to the extent that Solomon "was wiser than any other man" (1 Kings 4:31). When the Queen of Sheba heard about "the fame of Solomon and his relation to the name of the Lord" (1 Kings 10:1), she visited him and tested him with difficult questions. After receiving detailed and logical answers and seeing his great buildings and accomplishments she praised God (not Solomon!) and recognized that He had placed Solomon on the throne of Israel. His wisdom pointed her to God's greatness.

In the same way, people who practice righteousness, justice and fairness in all areas of their lives—sports, friendships, homework or jobs—help others see that God lives in them and gives them an increasing degree of common sense in these matters. Instead of making arbitrary, selfish decisions Christians go out of their way to be fair and helpful. They see the other side of the issue; they can admit they're wrong and make amends. Just as the Queen of Sheba tested Solomon, non-Christians may test Christians with doctrinal questions or difficult situations; and they may come to recognize the Christians' wisdom as a gift from God. We should respond to these tests with gentleness instead of irritation, and then rejoice that someone noticed our witness (see 1 Pet. 3:15).

Being different doesn't have to make us odd or peculiar, but we can be a better sort of "different" that people appreciate as they come to rely on our character. We should be honored if our friends don't invite us to join them in questionable activities, or if they say, "I didn't think you'd want to go, but I just thought I'd ask." They respect us and will remember to include us in the worthwhile activities.

Does our behavior advertise that we are Christians? Does our righteousness, justice or fairness stand out? As we abide in God, this uncommon wisdom grows and bursts forth as fruit of that growth.

Read Proverbs 1:3. Underline any elements of wisdom that you need to acquire. As you examine your relationships with friends and family for signs of righteousness, justice and fairness, review verses in Proverbs from this book that contain the wisdom you need.

Day 2 Confidence in Witnessing

We've all heard sayings like these: "Why doesn't he practice what he preaches?" "What she does speaks so loudly that I can't hear what she's saying!" . . . or, "I'd rather see a sermon in shoes than hear a lecture from a Christian." Sometimes we're afraid to speak up for Christ because someone might make one of these remarks about us!

Timothy may have had a similar problem, for Paul encouraged him not to let others look down on him because of his youthfulness. Instead Paul advised him to confidently present an example to them in speech, life, love, faith and purity (see 1 Tim. 4:12). What a tall order! But once again, wisdom comes to the rescue by providing confidence. Proverbs teaches that one who "fears the Lord" has a "secure fortress" (Prov. 14:26, *NIV*), or "strong confidence" (Prov. 14:26, *NKJV*).

How does wisdom provide confidence? First, wise people trust the Lord to protect them: "When you walk, your steps will not be hampered; when you run, you will not stumble" (Prov. 4:12). God provides clear paths for those who attempt to share the gospel. Trusting God removes the burden of scheming to witness to others. God should be in charge of the when, where, how and who of witnessing. Proverbs says that when we commit whatever we do to the Lord, He's responsible for the outcome (see Prov. 16:3). We may set the goal in witnessing by praying for a friend but God directs the steps by providing opportunities and motivation.

Second, the one who gets wisdom "loves his own soul" (Prov. 19:8). This is not conceit, but doing what is best for the object of love—in this case, oneself. Wisdom provides the necessary security to relieve us from our self-consciousness so that our first concern is no longer what others think of us, but what others will think of God and His kingdom. We willingly put our reputations on the line to enhance God's reputation. Because God has helped us, we want to share that with others so that they will benefit too.

Third, the wise know what to do when they fail to practice what they preach. Wise Christians are in the process of learning humility which frees them to take the steps God advises: (1) accepting rebuke without scoffing (see Prov. 15:31); (2) confessing their sins and renouncing them (see Prov. 28:13). We all know people who cannot admit that they are wrong, but we admire people who are secure enough to admit it and to correct what they have done. In fact this attitude is so rare that it can strengthen our Christian witness: it helps others know that we don't think we are perfect, but just growing in the Lord.

Witnessing is a scary proposition. Through it, God teaches us to trust Him for confidence. Self-confidence will fail us, but God-confidence will boost our abilities beyond what we ever thought possible.

What is the source of your confidence?

Do you feel secure enough to witness?

Can you admit you're wrong? Review the verses mentioned in this reading and ask God to reorganize your thoughts about yourself. Choose a friend or relative and pray that God will make your life's example a positive witness to that person.

Day 3 The Witness of Reverence

Gina and Julie were tense with anticipation as they approached the amusement park. As they stood before the roller coaster Gina suddenly grew pale and declared that she would not ride it. Julie, though recognizing the risks involved, decided to ride the monstrous structure. Out of the millions who pass through the turnstiles at amusement parks, many people possess a healthy respect for the roller coaster's colossal power and potential danger, but they still choose to ride. Why do some fear roller coasters and others delight in them? Some do not trust the safety of the ride. Others have confidence that the ride is safe. They abide by the rules and enjoy the experience.

What is the difference between fear and respect? Which feeling most resembles your attitude toward God? When the writer of Proverbs recommended that believers be "zealous for the fear of the Lord" (Prov. 23:17) he referred to an awe or reverence for God rather than terror of Him. This reverence for God teaches us wisdom and produces confidence, contentment, life, wealth and honor (see Prov. 15:33; 14:26; 19:23; 22:4).

These positive effects of "fearing the Lord" prove God's goodness by showing how He blesses us when we acknowledge His power and honor Him as God. When we cringe before God, we mislead others into thinking that God is solely a punisher of evil. But when we allow our love for God to drive out our natural fear of Him (see 1 John 4:18), we testify that a relationship between an infinite, perfect God and a finite, fallible human is attainable. Unbelievers find this possibility incredible and marvel that it can happen.

Think of a person you fear. Is your fear based on what the person is capable of doing to you? Do you distrust the power he or she holds over you? Reverence replaces fear when we trust a person's judgment or grow to love and admire him or her. By nature we shrink from God for He has the power to destroy us; but by building a relationship with Him through prayer and Bible study we discover that He loves us and wishes to do what is best for us. That knowledge of God enables us to love and respect Him instead of dreading Him.

The "fear of the Lord" aids our witness because it encompasses the hatred of evil, pride, arrogance, wrong behavior and perverse speech (see Prov. 8:13). The more we trust and reverence God, the more we view life from God's perspective—hating evil but caring for the one who participates in evil. Having a healthy distaste for evil motivates us to refrain from such behavior and produces a life of obvious witness in the midst of a society that readily accepts pride, arrogance and perverse speech. After a period of time others notice when we don't join in bragging, wrong behavior or profanity and even admire us as long as we avoid self-righteous pride and show acceptance of people.

To build a trusting reverence for God in your life, study the Scripture, praise Him in prayer and observe His power in your life and the lives of others. Note how God changes those who come to Him by helping them overcome sinful habits. As you study the Scripture, underline the phrase "fear of the Lord" every time it appears in Proverbs (more than fourteen times!). In the margin note if the verse defines "fear of the Lord" or names one of its effects. Think about the effects that you would like to see in your life and discuss them with God in prayer.

To develop a healthy respect for sin's power, be alert to Satan's strategies in your life. Observe his destructive influence upon others. Notice how he uses certain people or circumstances—or your own inclinations—to lead you astray and how he makes evil things look attractive. Observe those you know who gave in to one sin and then slid downhill into more and more sin.

Praise God for His power to keep you from sin and Satan's power.

Day 4 Using Encouragement to Witness

Eric enjoyed being a bagger at the supermarket—except for the obnoxious attitude of another bagger, Gary. Gary often tried to prove his strength and agility by carrying too many bags or bags that were too heavy—especially if the customer he was helping was an attractive girl. One day when Gary was showing off, as usual, he began to drop one of the bags just as the store manager was passing by. Eric was tempted to let Gary drop the bag, but instead he rescued Gary by catching the bag in such a way that the manager didn't even notice. When Eric, overcoming the temptation to rub it in, said nothing about the incident, Gary actually humbled himself enough to thank Eric and they became friends.

Proverbs abounds with verses that celebrate the encouraging person who offers cheerful looks, pleasant words, loyal friendship and practical help. The person who overcomes the temptation to be a grouchy complainer, and instead offers positive comments, ministers to both the body and the soul (see Prov. 15:30; 16:24). Amidst all of our self-centered talk, pleasant and encouraging words are a rare treat comparable to enjoying honey (see Prov. 16:24). Cheerful greetings and positive comments boost those around us who, unknown to us, may be suffering some defeat or loss. The writer of Hebrews advised us to concentrate "unswervingly" on the hope we profess in God who is unswervingly faithful! Because of that hope we should consider how we may spur one another on toward love and good deeds (see Heb. 10:23,24). Hope in God and the positive attitude it produces are contagious!

Going beyond words and expressions, a wise friend loves "at all times," even if a friend has done something foolish or damaging to his or her reputation. In fact, friendship is "born for adversity" (see Prov. 17:17) to help us get through the tough times. When others are putting us down, the wise encourager maintains the friendship and does what he or she can to help. Barnabas lived up to his name, "son of encouragement," by befriending Paul after his conversion when the other Christians understandably feared and mistrusted the former prosecutor (see Acts 9:26-31). An encourager dares to befriend those who need friends the most, despite others' comments. Like Barnabas, encouragers gradually win over the affections of the peer group for the outcast.

Wisdom even motivates us to encourage our enemies by giving them food and water when they need it. When the wise encourager sees people in such a spot, he or she seeks to meet their needs whether they're friends or enemies. This kind of overt love advertises the great love of God and enhances a believer's witness of Him.

How about the encouragers? They not only receive their reward from the Lord, but they also "find joy in giving an apt reply" and develop skill in "giving a timely word" (see Prov. 15:23).

Wouldn't you like to share a study hall or work at a hamburger stand with someone like that when you've blown an important test or been informed by a special friend that you're no longer special? That kind of life causes people to want to know more about God.

Skim through these Proverbs and notice the effects of quarrelsome, negative attitudes: 15:17; 17:1,14,22; 21:9,19; 26:21. If those verses describe you better than those about encouragers, decide today if you want the joy of giving encouragement to others and thus glorifying the Lord.

Day 5 Witness Through Patience

Patty lost her temper again—this time because Sue was a little late meeting her after school. Patty stomped off alone, trailing wreaths of anger and self-pity. Sue followed more slowly, praying for her friend. More than anything, Sue wanted Patty to come to know Christ.

The next day, typically, Patty apologized. She said, "I blew it again, Sue. I'm surprised you're still my friend. I do this all the time, but you don't seem to give up on me like other people do."

Sue replied, "I think you're a neat person. You have some rough edges, like your temper, but once you decide to let God help you, those will smooth out."

Sue demonstrated patience with her stormy friend. And patience, which is part of the fruit of the Holy Spirit (see Gal. 5:22,23), can be a tremendous witness.

We need to be patient with our friends who do not know Christ—patient with their character flaws and patient with their slowness in coming to Christ. We Christians need to be the ones who don't give up on them when everyone else does—and the people who demonstrate our belief that they can be "somebodies." Someday when they want to know more about the meaning of life, they will remember that the Christians were the ones who stuck with them.

We also need to be patient with God. Does that sound a bit strange? Think about it. How often do we Christians get frustrated because things are not going our way? Our friends aren't receiving Christ, our prayers "aren't answered," our circumstances are not what we want them to be. Maybe the people at school who cheat on tests are getting better grades and more respect than we are, despite our hard work and strict honesty.

All sorts of things like those mentioned can make us impatient with the way God runs things. And that impatience is bound to show, even if we don't admit it out loud.

We need to realize two things about God. The first is that His thoughts are not like our thoughts (see Isa. 55:8,9). He is wiser than we are, and He knows more than we do. He can see the outcome of an action while we are still thinking about the short-term gratification it will bring us. He knows what is really good for us—which is often far from what we *think* is good for us.

The second thing we need to realize is that God has for us a goal higher than merely our happiness or enjoyment. He is trying to build character, to make us more like Christ (see Rom. 5:3-5; 8:28,29). Since He is a loving Father, He wants to give us as much happiness as possible—but not to the extent that it will interfere with our growth. And sometimes we have to suffer a little or a lot in order to grow. If we are patient with God in those times of difficulty, if we trust Him to be doing the right thing even when it's something that hurts, then our witness for Him will shine all the brighter.

Check out the verses below and think about your need to be patient with people and patient with God.

Proverbs 19:11; Colossians 3:12-14; Isaiah 55:8,9; Romans 5:3-5; James 5:7,8.

Day 6 Protecting Our Witness

"They don't make them like they used to," mused the sports announcer, reminiscing about the days when football players wore a minimal amount of protective padding. The equipment now in use protects today's football "gladiators" from injuries to vital organs and muscles essential to achieving a successful performance on the playing field.

We often feel as vulnerable as a football player without helmet or padding when we think about speaking of Christ to strangers, friends or family members. Proverbs informs us that *pursuing wisdom* helps insure an effective witness: "Do not forsake wisdom, and she will protect you; love her, and she will watch over you" (Prov. 4:6). Grasping God's wisdom helps us to resist temptation of all kinds which might damage our witness. For example, reading about giving a soft, gentle answer to turn away wrath (see Prov. 15:1) prepares us to deal with the quarrelsome sophomore in the lunch line and thus show a stronger witness to friends. Seekers of wisdom build their own spiritual "football equipment"—righteousness, justice and fairness—by learning God's "plays" (commands) and "huddling" with other Christians.

In order to build this protection, Proverbs advises us to *lay hold* of God's words with all our heart, not to forget them and then to keep them (see Prov. 4:4,5). This involves studying His commands, thinking about them and practicing them. As other interests press us, we find we must guard instruction (see Prov. 4:13) by setting aside time to study God's Word, to pray about putting it into practice, and to serve Him. We must view His commands as a lamp to our life (see Prov. 6:23) without which we easily fall into temptation.

Proverbs also mentions that many advisors insure victory (see 11:14). Through "huddle" experiences such as Bible study, worship and youth activities, you can build a fellowship with Christian students and adults who can help you maintain a wise perspective on life and plan strategies for attacking sin. That's not to say that we must associate only with other Christians, but that we should look to Christians as our examples and advisors. This continuous quest for wisdom helps us evaluate ourselves and build a testimony that praises God.

Do you regularly read God's Word and fellowship with other Christians? Proverbs promises rewards for pursuing wisdom besides the protection it gives our souls. Examine Proverbs 6:24; 15:9; and 13:14 for rewards that accompany this search.

S.H.

I
HATE
WITNESSING

If deep down in your guts
you feel this way too—
don't miss the new book
I Hate Witnessing
coming soon from the
Light Force!